CARING FOR CREATION

TOGETHER

Emma Major

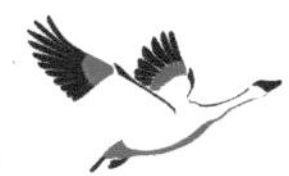

wild goose
publications

www.**iona**books.com

First published 2022 by
Wild Goose Publications,
Suite 9, Fairfield, 1048 Govan Road, Glasgow G51 4XS, Scotland
the publishing division of the Iona Community.
Scottish Charity No. SC003794. Limited Company Reg. No. SC096243.

ISBN 978-1-80432-000-6

The publishers gratefully acknowledge the support of the Drummond Trust,
3 Pitt Terrace, Stirling FK8 2EY in producing this book.

Overseas distribution:
Australia: Willow Connection Pty Ltd, Unit 4A, 1/13 Kell Mather Drive, Lennox Head NSW 2478
New Zealand: Pleroma, Higginson Street, Otane 4170, Central Hawkes Bay

Printed by Ashford Colour Press, Gosport, UK

CARING FOR CREATION

TOGETHER

Emma Major

Introduction

This set of 40 paintings and poems was created during Lent 2021. Each morning I spent time with God: reading the Bible, praying, pondering and painting. I didn't have an aim in mind. I didn't expect to 'produce' anything. I just sought the peace that painting and praying brings me.

Every day I found myself coming back to the impact of climate change on the planet, issues of climate justice on the most vulnerable in our world and the impending climate emergency.

The paintings each emerged differently. Sometimes I would be inspired by colour, sometimes by shapes or marks. Sometimes the haiku would come first and inspire the painting. Usually the painting would 'show' me something which inspired the poem, such as a fish choking on rubbish, a penguin, a crocodile, icebergs melting, or figures in prayer.

I didn't set out to create a series. I didn't even realise my daily creativity had become a series until I sat and looked through my paintings and poems at Easter. Only then, on Easter Day, was it obvious to me that God had inspired this creative response to the climate emergency. Only then did I realise that these could be used to raise more awareness of climate justice.

Over the next few weeks I asked a few trusted friends what they thought of the paintings and poems and how they might be useful. A series of ideas rapidly emerged from these conversations, and in the past six months the set has become: an exhibition at St Nicolas Church, Earley; a digital installation in Reading Minster Church of St Mary the Virgin launching the Young Christian Climate Network residency as part of their Relay to COP26; a set of cards to inspire prayer, share with others or even send to politicians asking them to take action on climate justice issues; an exhibition as part of the Great Big Green Week, 2021. And as I write this, the original set of paintings and poems is being prepared to travel to Glasgow to go on display at COP26, hosted by, and raising money for, Tearfund.

My hope is that these paintings and poems might help people to engage with the reality of climate change in a way they haven't before.

Maybe the set about animals will move someone to reduce their individual impact on the planet.

Maybe the set about the need to work together will inspire someone to join an action group or make a change in their place of work.

Maybe the paintings and poems will help people to pray, or create, or be chosen by a book group, or used in a church service, or in a Lenten discipline, or given as a gift …

I don't know.

I just trust that since God gave them to me in my prayer time that they must be meant to make a difference somehow.

Emma Major

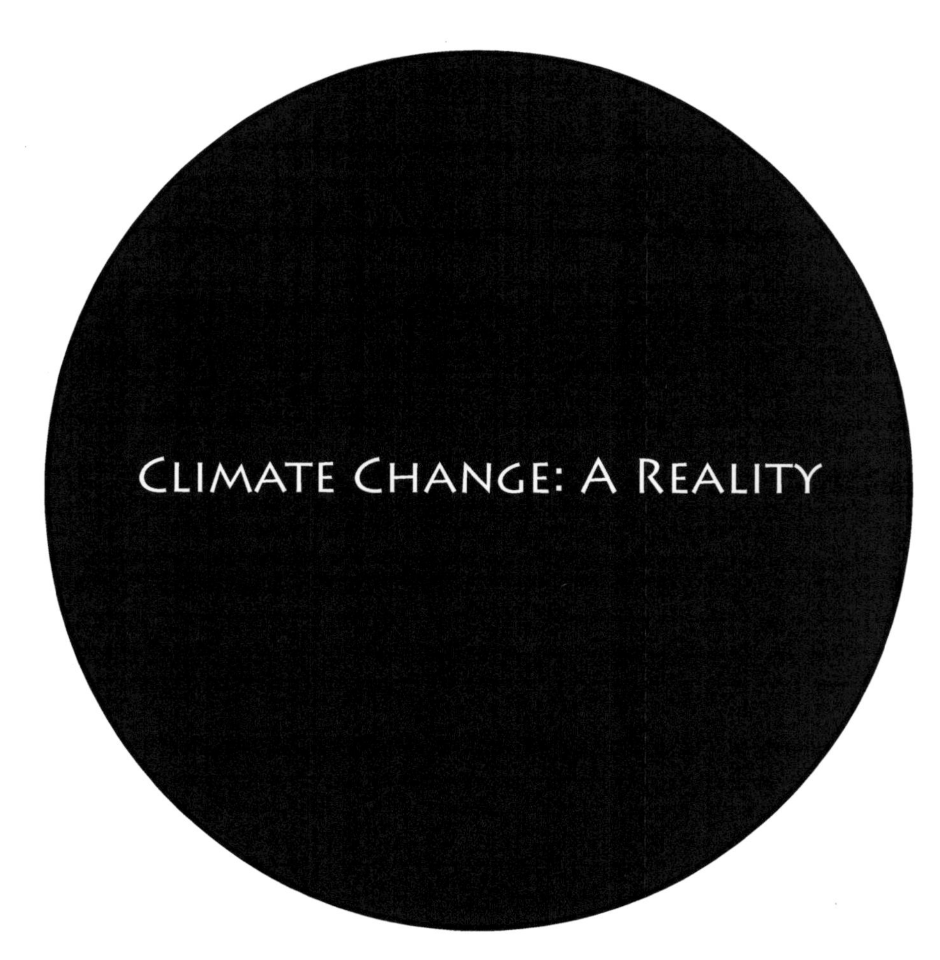
CLIMATE CHANGE: A REALITY

The UN has declared a climate emergency.

There is still time to act – but it must happen immediately.

This first set of paintings and poems raises some of the realities of climate change and challenges us to think about how we can all make a difference.

Creator God,
inspire nations, organisations
and individuals
to implement the changes needed
to halt climate change.

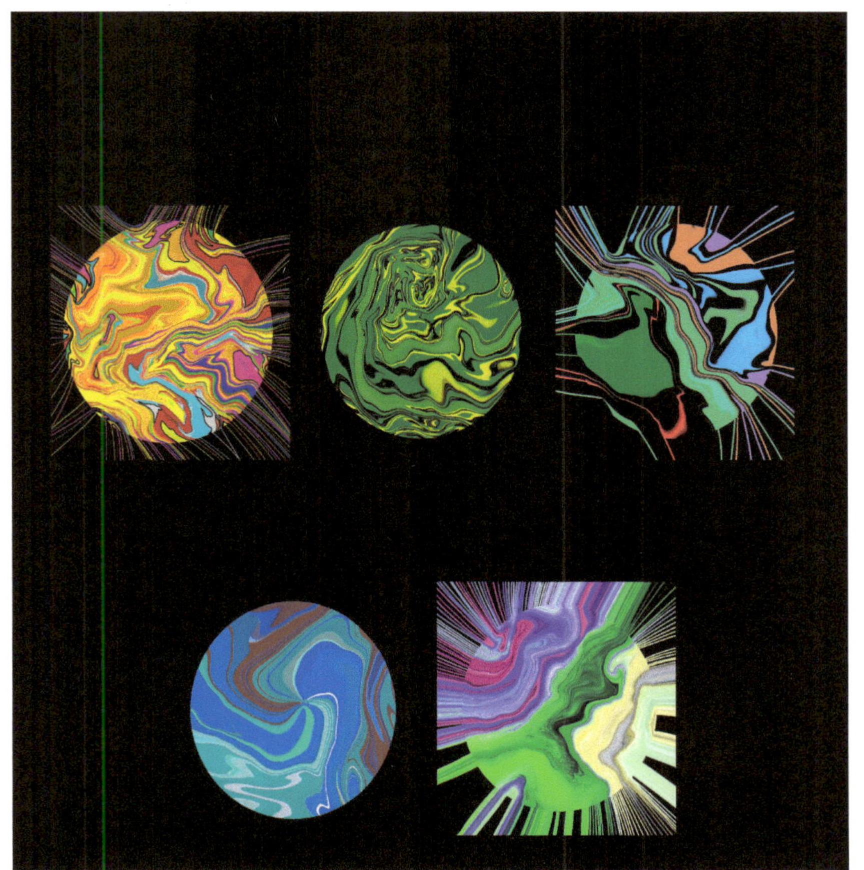

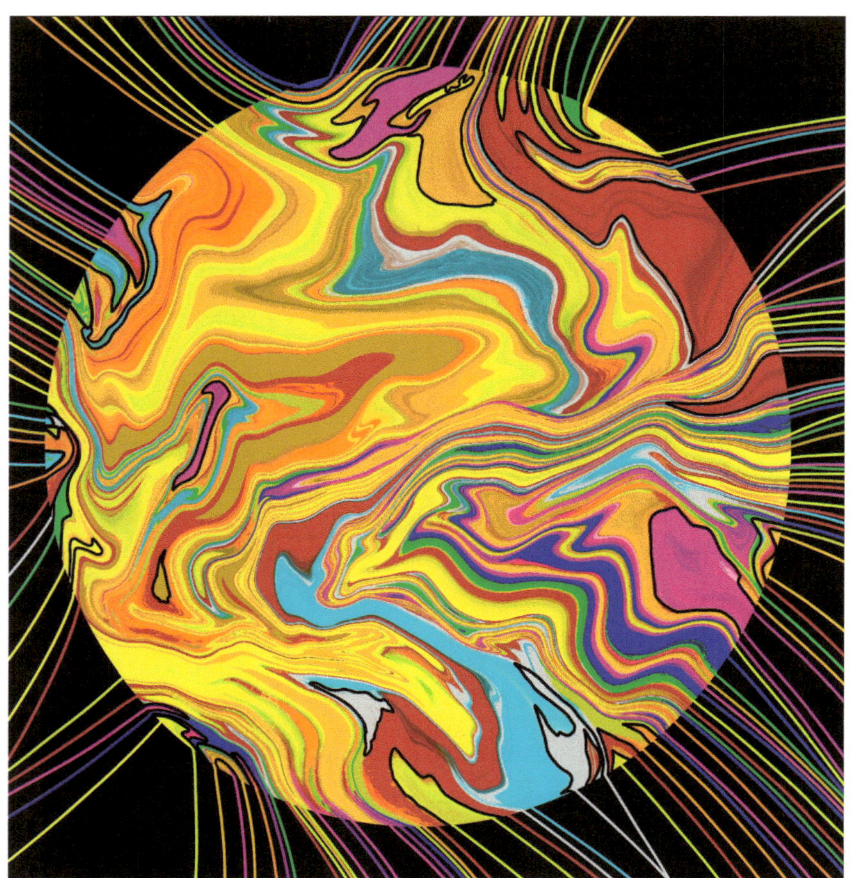

A lot of hot air
Around climate change issues
Whilst the ice caps melt

Countries, businesses, charities and churches around the world have been 'declaring a climate emergency'. The words are good; but an emergency needs more than words – it needs action.

In November 2021, COP26 brought together members of governments from across the world to make plans to deal with the climate emergency. Post-COP26, let's keep asking those in power to act quickly.

No diversity
Farming too intensively
Future scarcity

Whenever I speak about this painting, I call it 'Sad planet'. It may look alive and well, with several shades of green and shots of yellow, perhaps a field of corn; but let's ask ourselves what's missing.

Where are the field poppies, marigolds and colourful hedgerows teeming with life?

What does this painting say to you?

How does it make you feel?

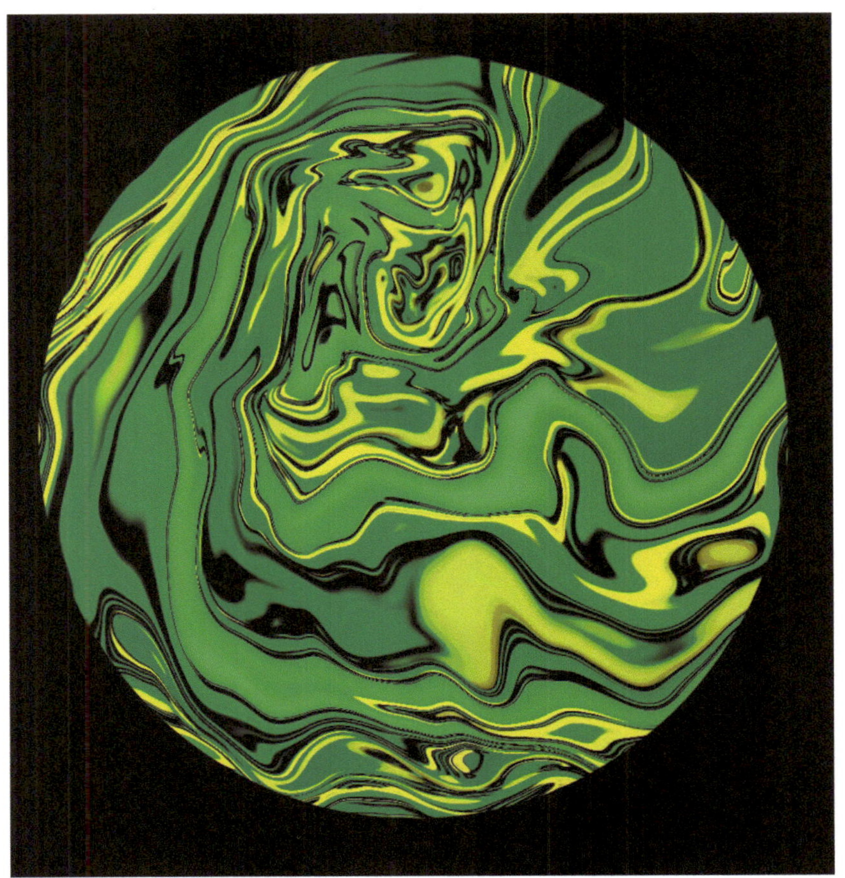

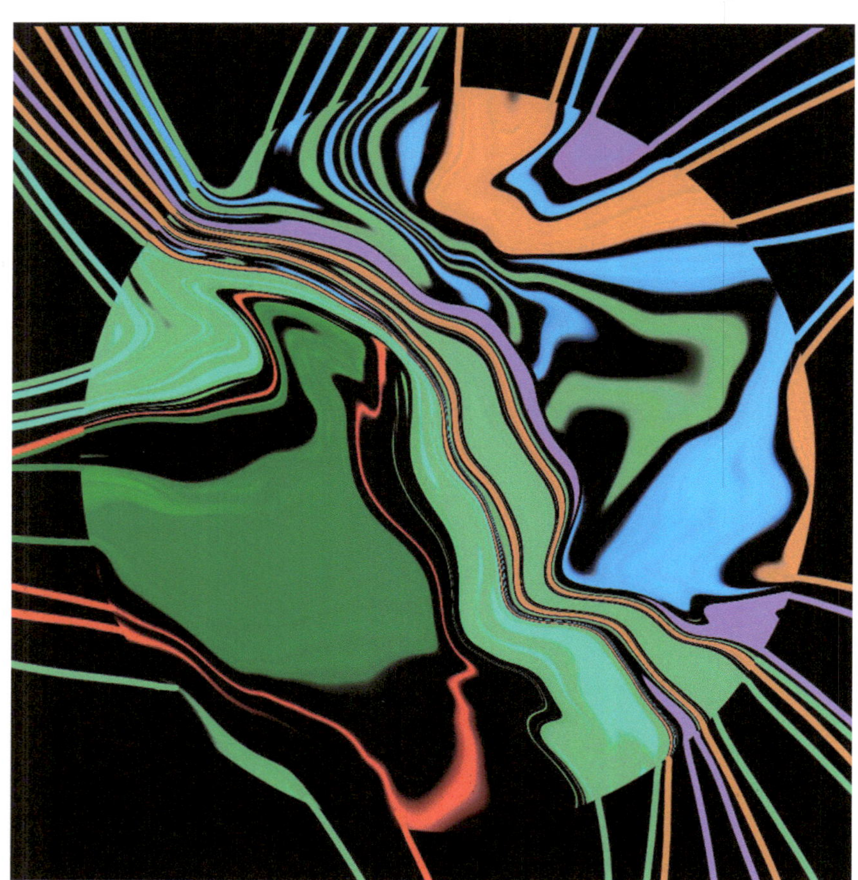

Wide-ranging species
Any possibility
Of diversity

If the previous painting was a sad planet, then this is a happy planet.

When areas of habitat are allowed to re-wild then they become much more diverse in the species of plants and animals found there – full of colour and movement. Life.

Diversity is essential for the natural balance of the earth.

How could you help to diversify your part of the world?

Swimming in circles
Repeating the same mistakes
Will we ever learn?

Round and round and round they go,
trying to look conscientious without
affecting their profit margins.

Which organisations should we hold to
account?

What actions can we take to make it clear
to those in power that we demand
change?

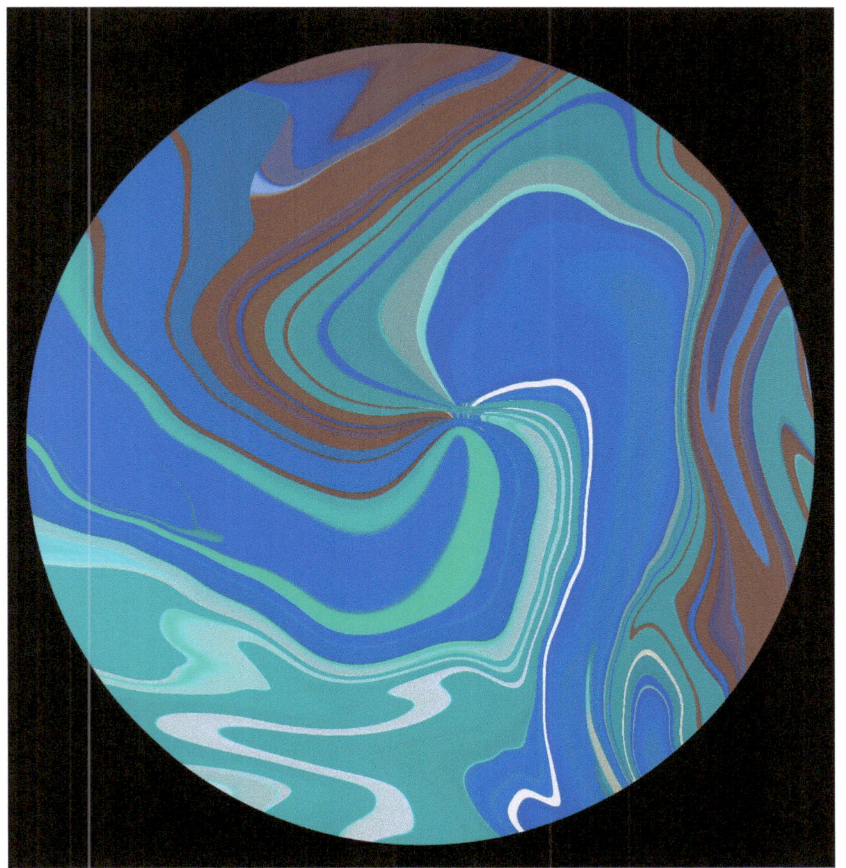

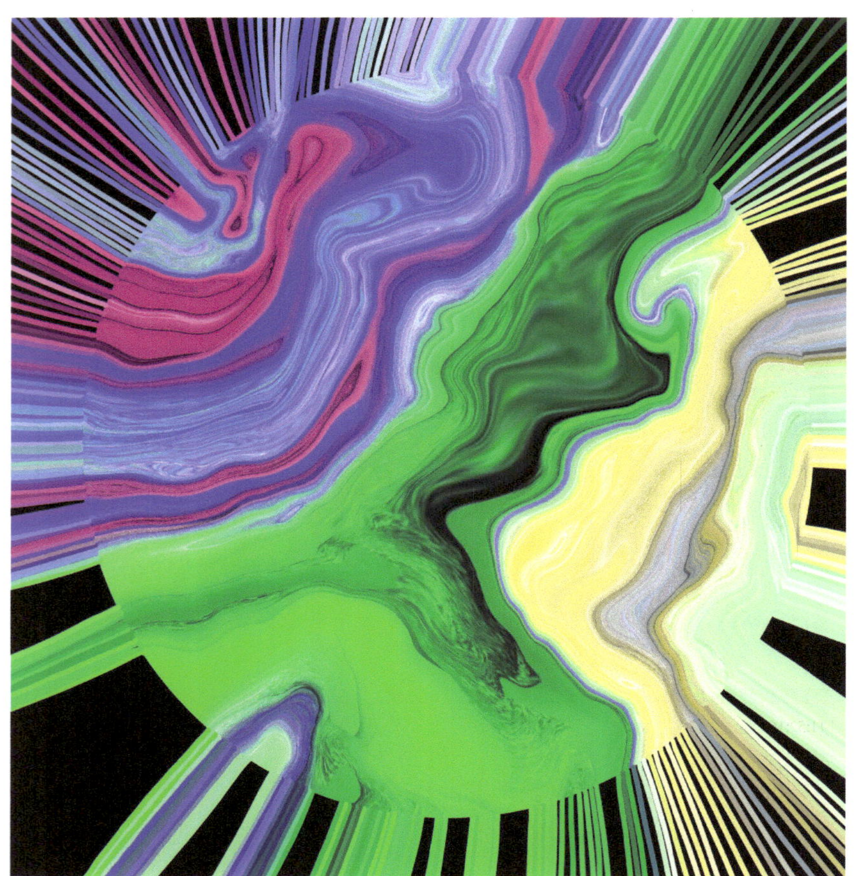

Climate is changing
Explosive reality
Approaching at speed

I love the vibrancy of this painting; I remember gasping out loud when I finished creating it. Yet it spoke to me about the emergency we are facing, the risk that we have pushed this beautiful, life-filled planet to its limit.

I pray that this is not the case, that changes will be implemented and the climate emergency tackled for the good of future generations.

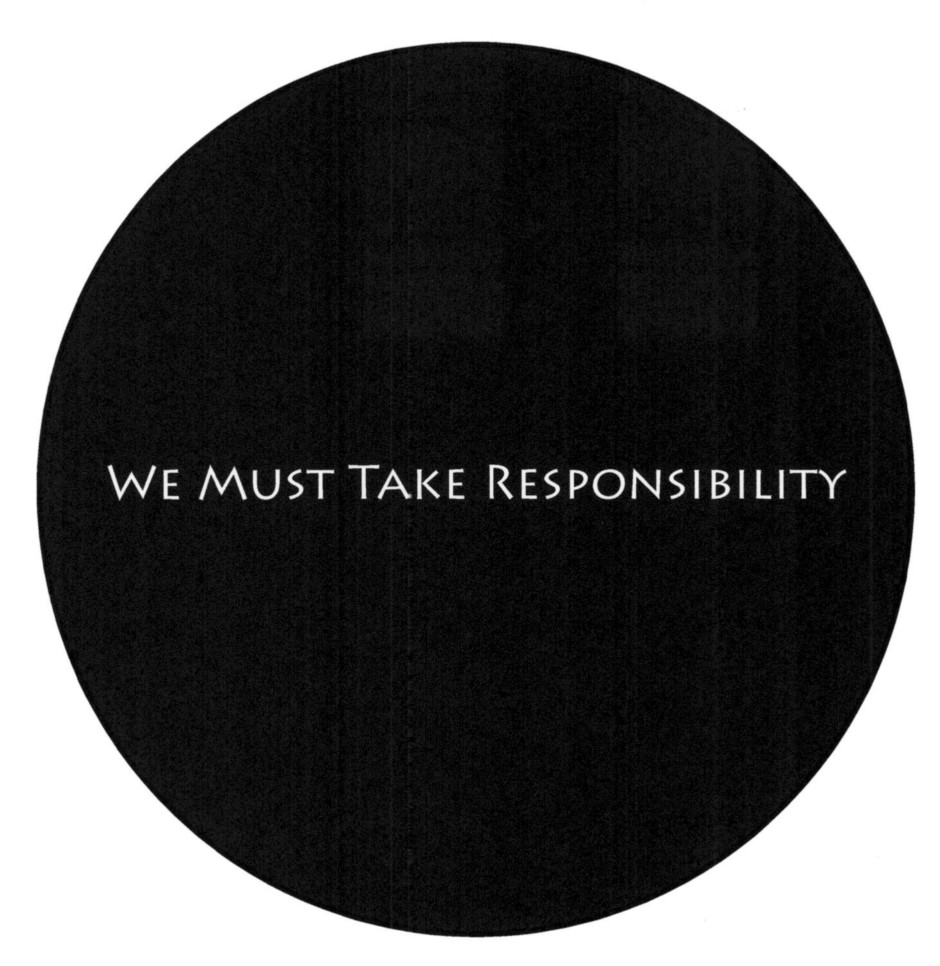
We Must Take Responsibility

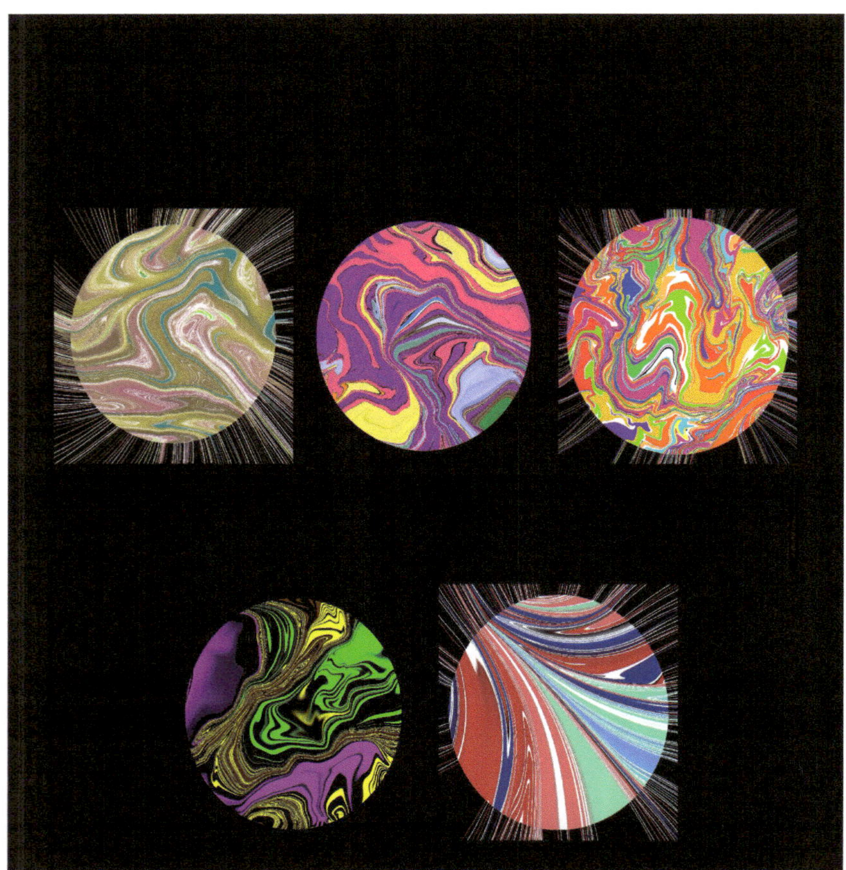

We must take responsibility: not you, not them, but us, all of us – together.

Together we can be a force for positive change; together we can help those in power to realise that they must change.

Creator God,
guide our time, words and actions
to make a difference in the world,
before it's too late.

Billions of beings
Living harmoniously
Giving selflessly

This painting speaks to me of the delicate balance of life in all its complexity, and the impact of human beings on that precious balance.

We must reduce our impact as a species in order to sustain life on earth.

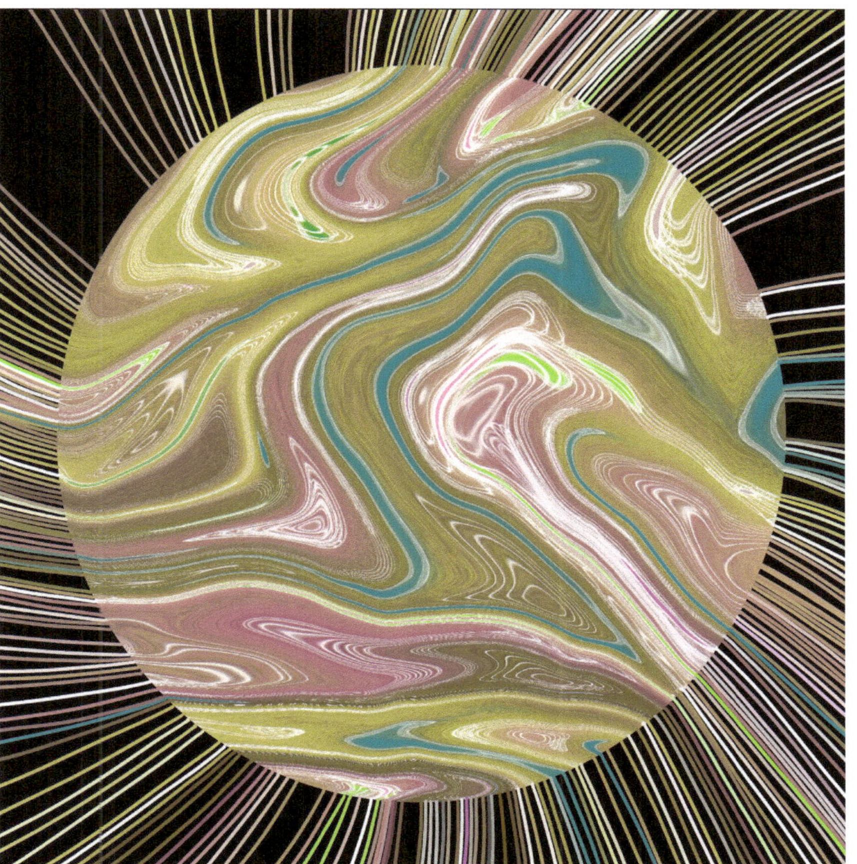

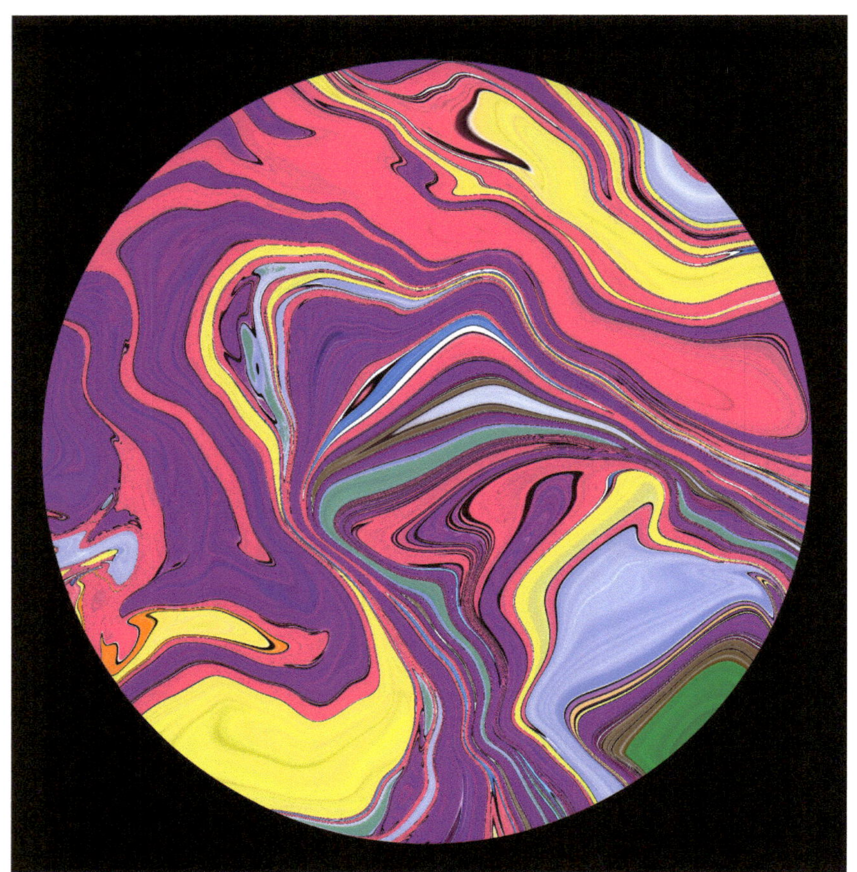

What really matters
In the greatest scheme of things
It should be nature

What issues take up most of your bandwidth?

How much of your attention, conversations and prayers is given to climate justice? God has tasked us to care for the earth and for all that lives upon it.

How do you feel when you spend time in nature?

Hot spots of damage
Dislocated from the cause
Harm beyond our sight

It can be hard to imagine the scale of deforestation around the world. We are disconnected from the damage.

So I have made a concerted effort to find stories about people and places affected by climate change. Doing this has helped me to see the benefit of every positive action I take, no matter how small.

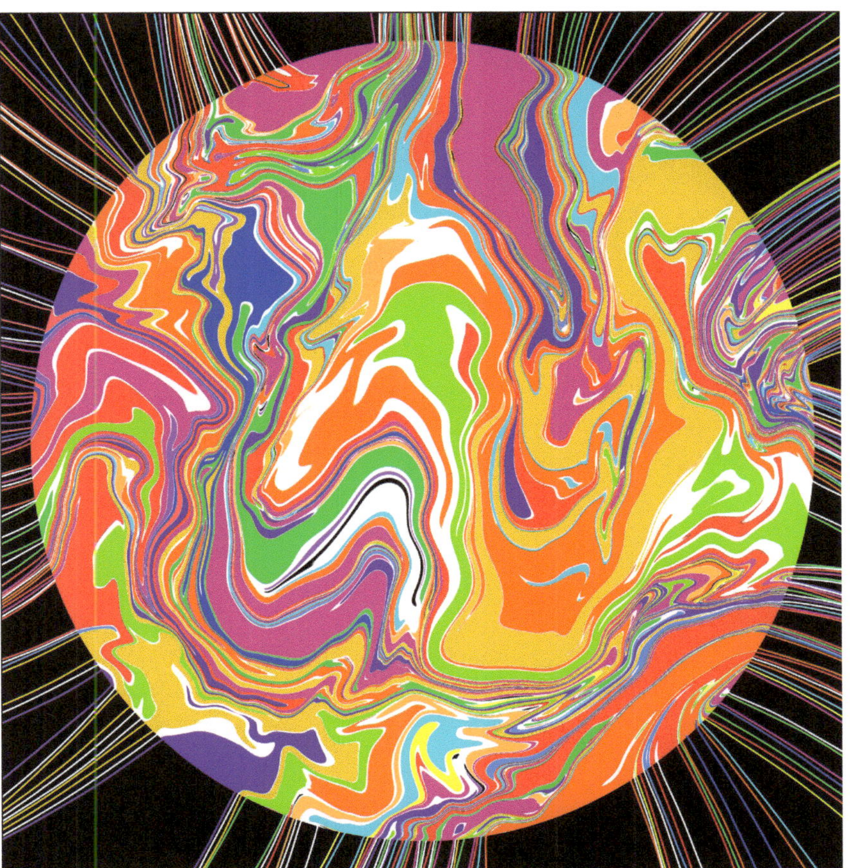

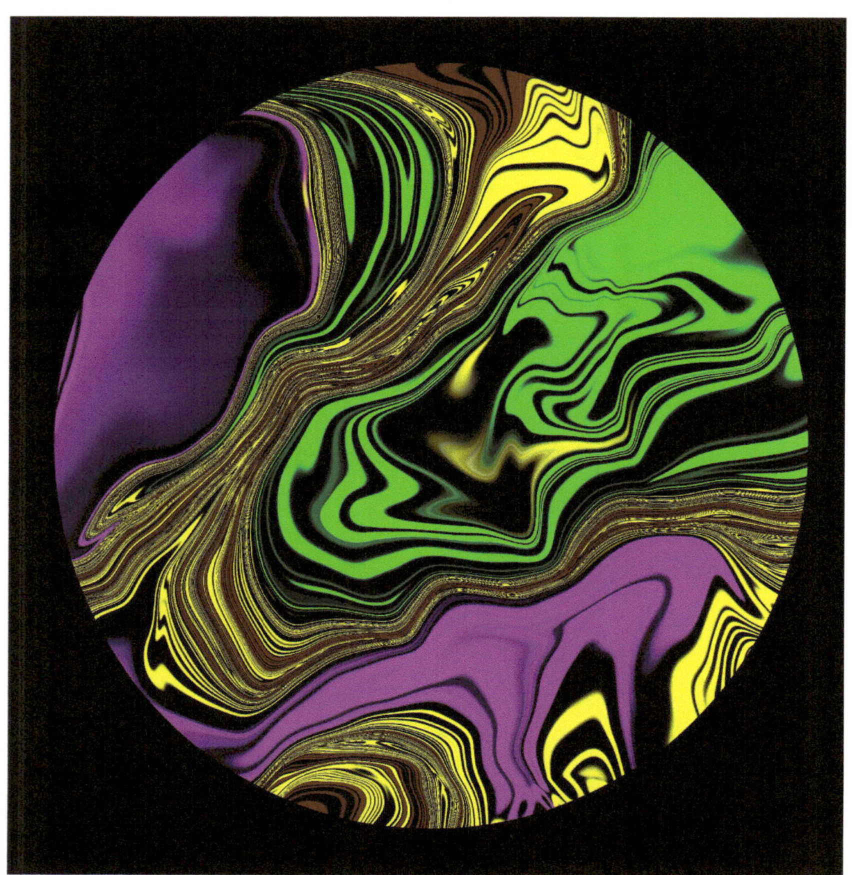

Do we choose wisely?
All actions have reactions
Recycle, reuse

Recycling was almost unheard of a decade ago, and yet now it's just part of life. Five years ago we couldn't imagine how we'd cope without being given a bag with our shopping, now we all carry a reusable bag with us. Two years ago it seemed very strange to carry a reusable cup or bottle with us, now we all do it.

What other small actions can we all take to make a huge difference to the planet?

Slippery slopes
Is there any turning back?
Climate action now

It's not too late, but it's getting close.
Those in power need to take action now,
right now.

Have you written to your MP to say you
expect them to take action?

Can you change to sustainable forms of
energy? What else could you do? …

It's not too late, but it's getting close.

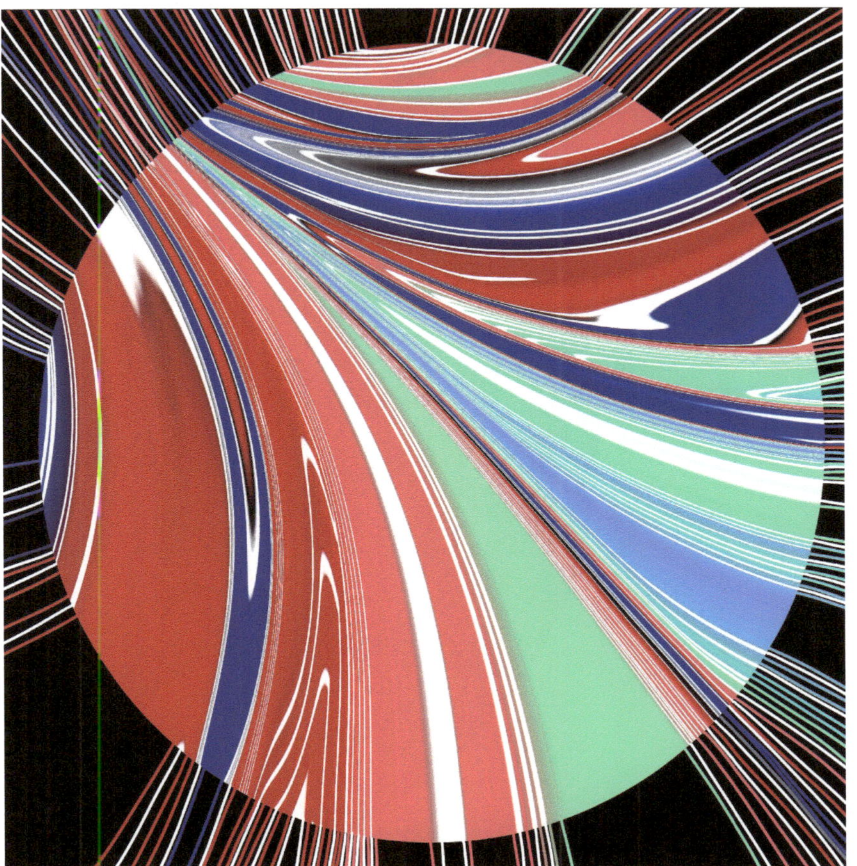

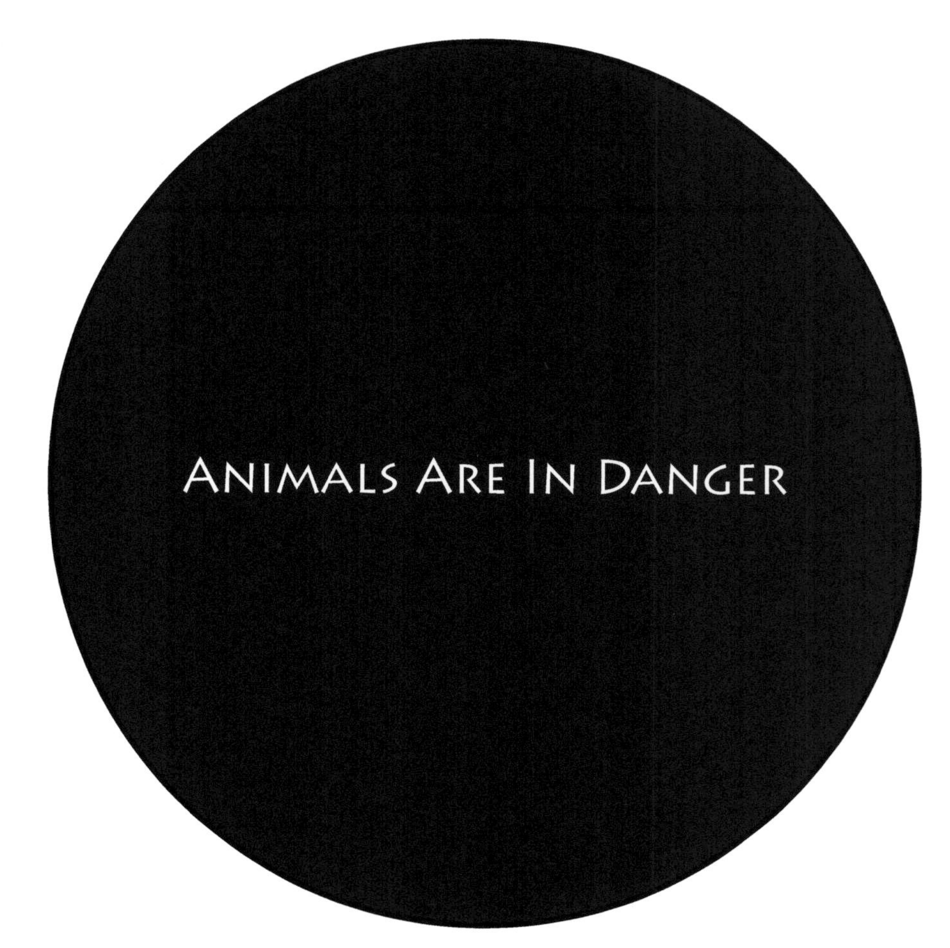

Animals Are In Danger

The Sir David Attenborough effect has been incredible. The way he speaks about climate change and shows its impact on animals around the world has had a huge impact on people's awareness of the issues.

This set of paintings and poems is my small contribution to raising awareness of the effects of climate change on animals around the world.

Creator God,
remind us that every action we take
has an effect, for good or bad,
on animals across the globe;
help us to reduce our negative impact.

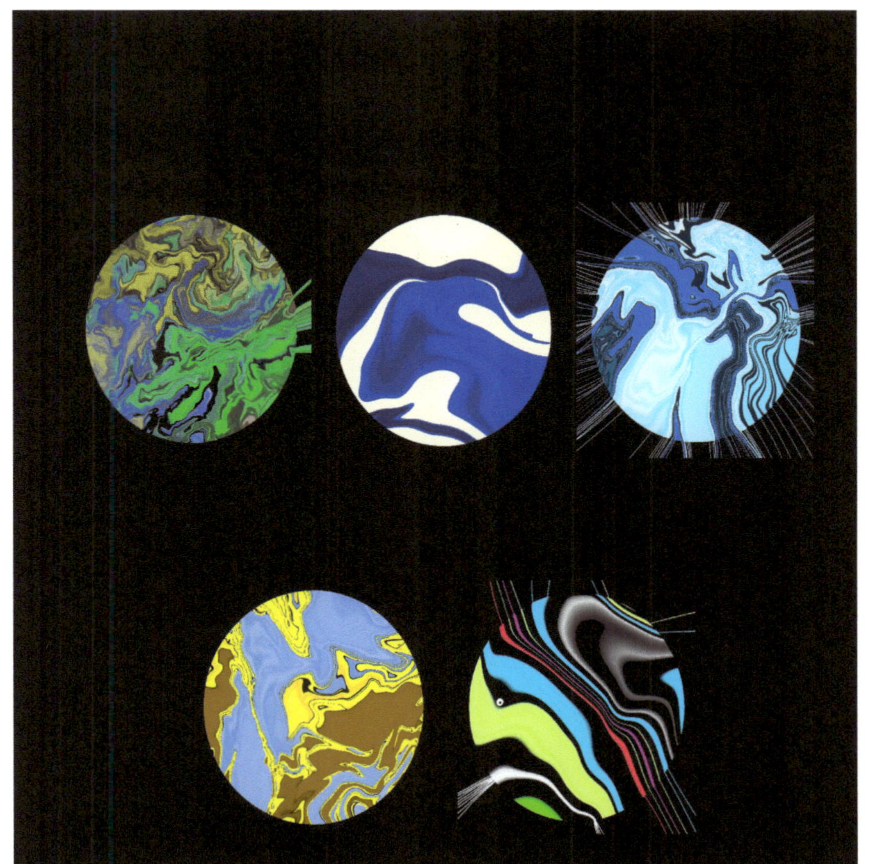

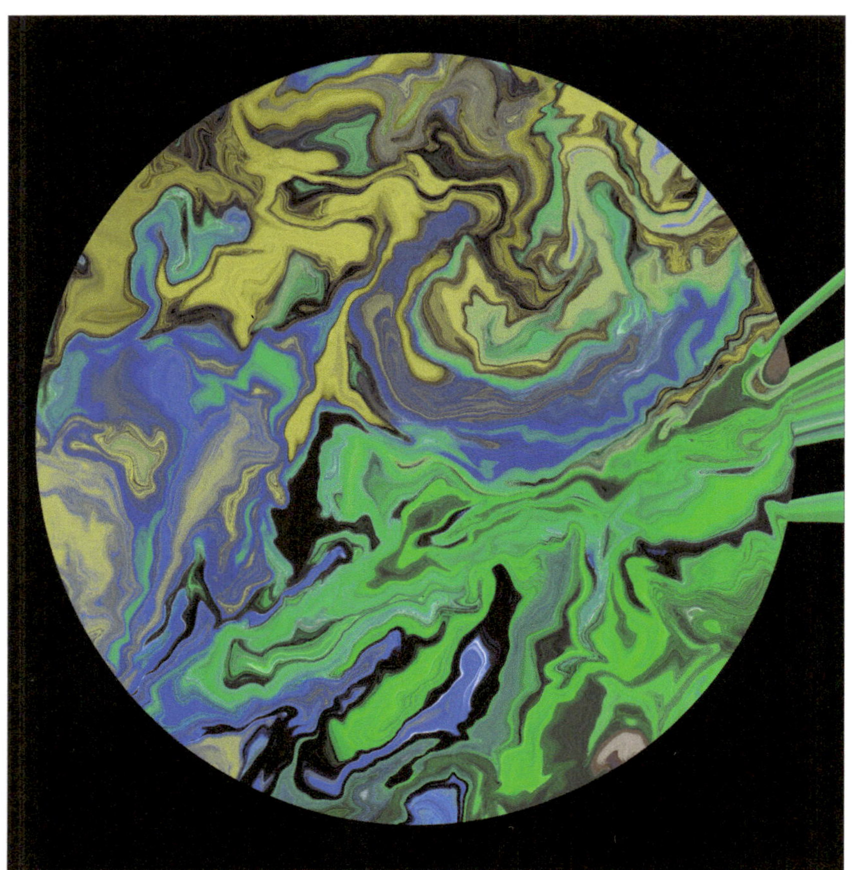

As water gets warm
Genders of crocodiles change
Too many males

I know this sounds made up but I promise you it's not. Whether a crocodile egg becomes male or female is determined by the temperature of the egg during its lifespan. As the planet warms up, the balance of male and female crocodiles is changing and this is affecting the reproduction rate.

Might our children see the extinction of one of the oldest species on earth?

Warming sea melts ice
Killer whales advancing north
Narwhals now at risk

Arctic Ocean temperatures are rising due to global warming and the sea ice is reducing. These changes are affecting the food supply for narwhals. And the narwhals are also now at risk from killer whales, which are migrating further north as waters warm.

The delicate balance of ecosystems is changing with untold consequences.

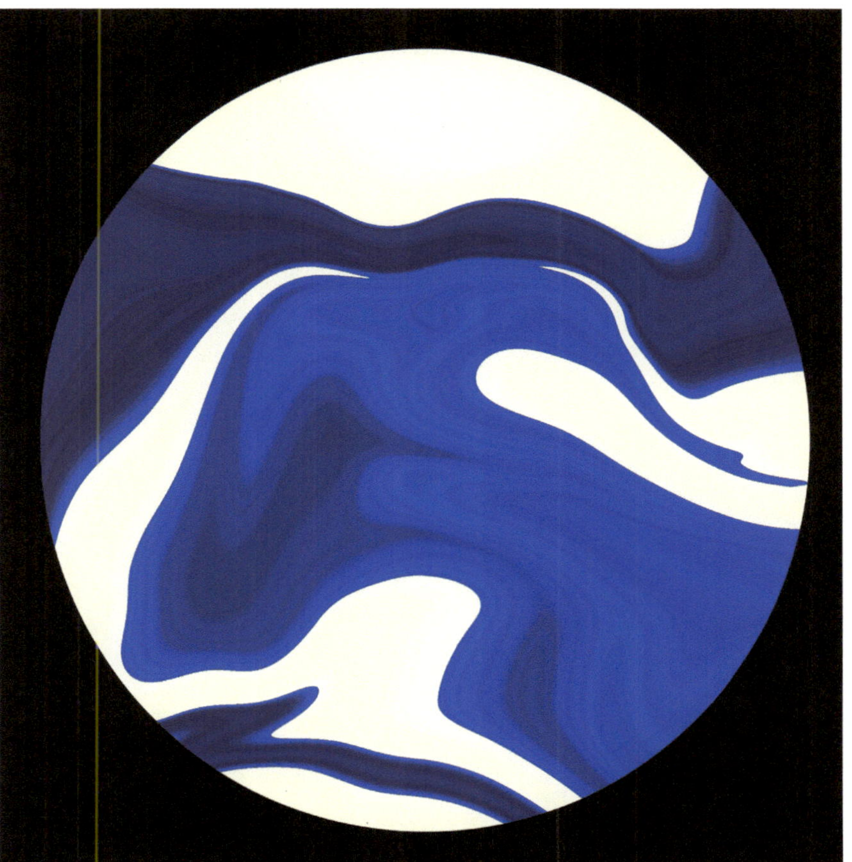

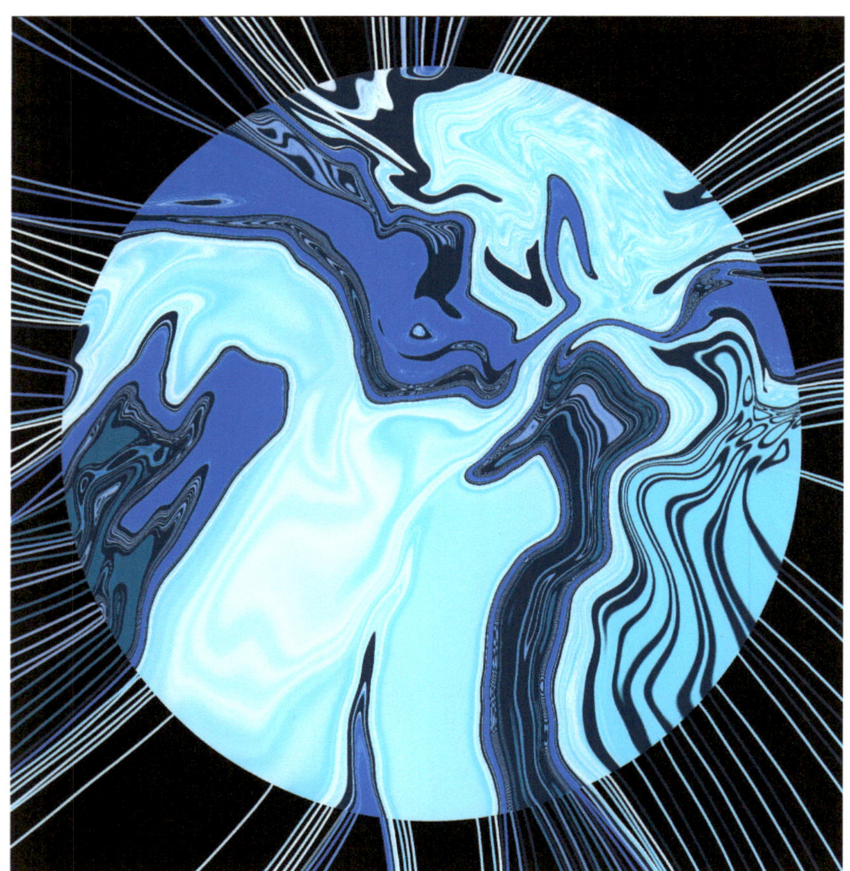

*Penguins losing ice
Climate change endangering
Every living thing*

From the Arctic, we travel to the other end of the world where the Antarctic ice sheet is also reducing due to rising temperatures and the snow is turning to rain. These are just two of the impacts of climate change on the different species of penguins there. I can see a penguin in this painting. Can you?

Every action we take has an effect, for good or bad, across the globe.

When dinosaurs roamed
Might alligators have dreamed
They'd face extinction?

Can you see the pterodactyl in this painting? It jumped out at me and inspired the haiku. Alligators roamed the planet with the dinosaurs, but now they are threatened by warming temperatures.

This is bad enough in itself but the extinction of an apex predator would have a profound negative impact on the habitats they leave behind.

Our actions are causing this.

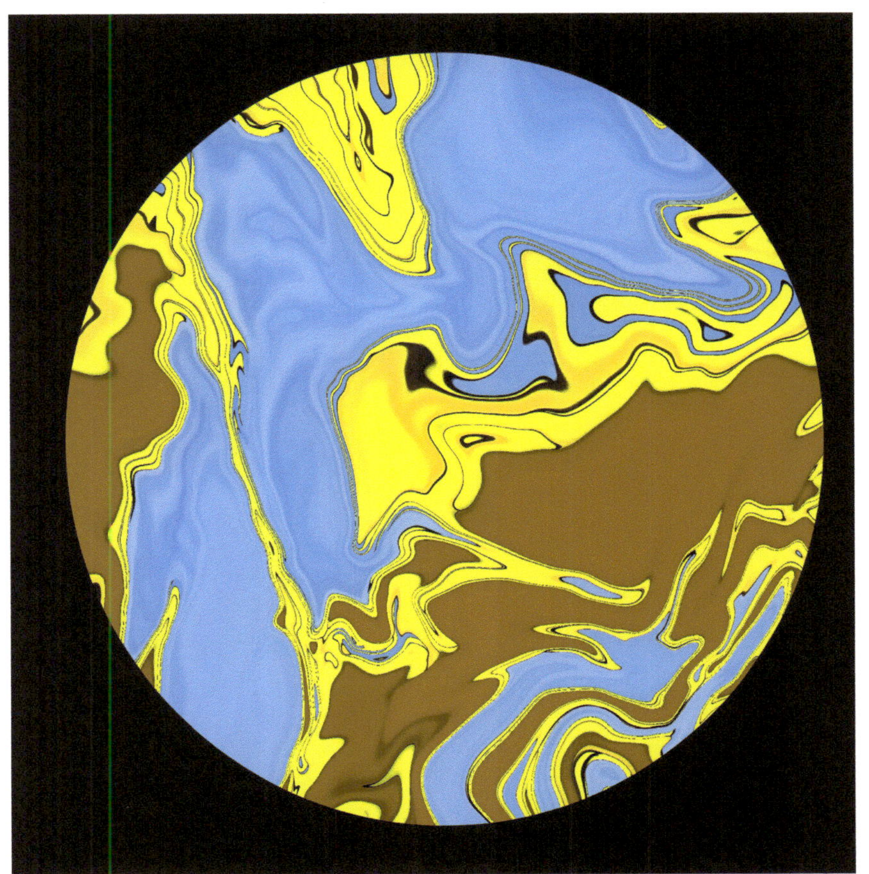

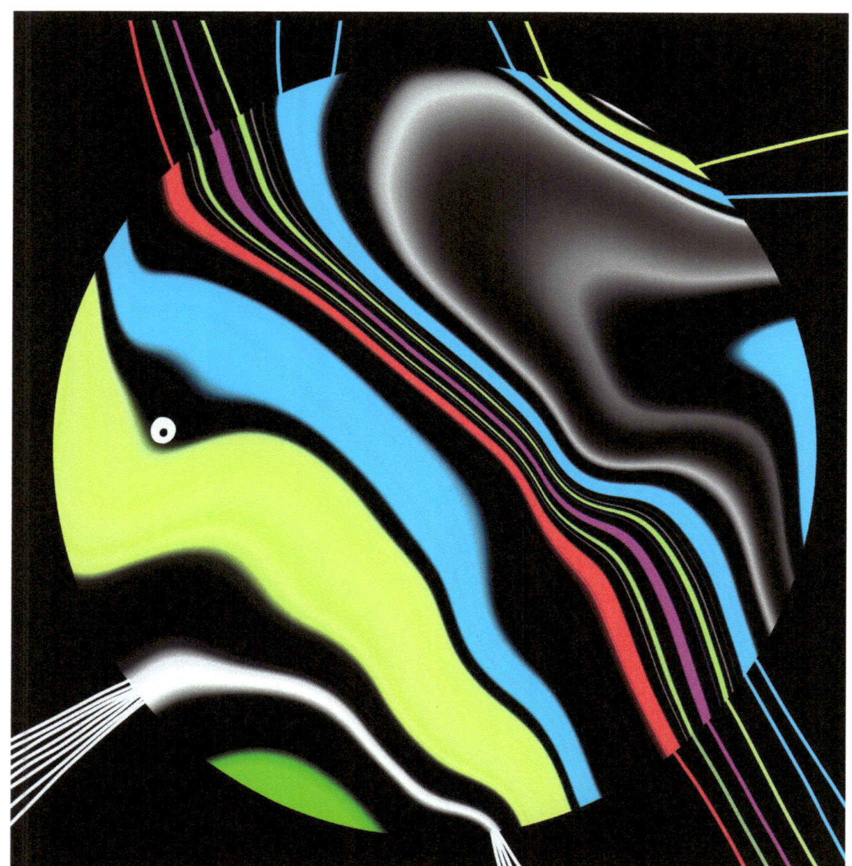

Plastic-filled oceans
Endangering wildlife
Time to really change

As I painted this, a fish appeared and then an open mouth, and from then on all I could see was a fish with rubbish in its mouth.

Do you see it? No one could remain unmoved by the pictures of floating rubbish in our oceans. It has brought about a change away from single-use plastics but there is more action needed to ensure our rubbish doesn't end up in the oceans.

When you visit a beach, lake, river or stream do you pick up the rubbish you find? Small actions make a difference.

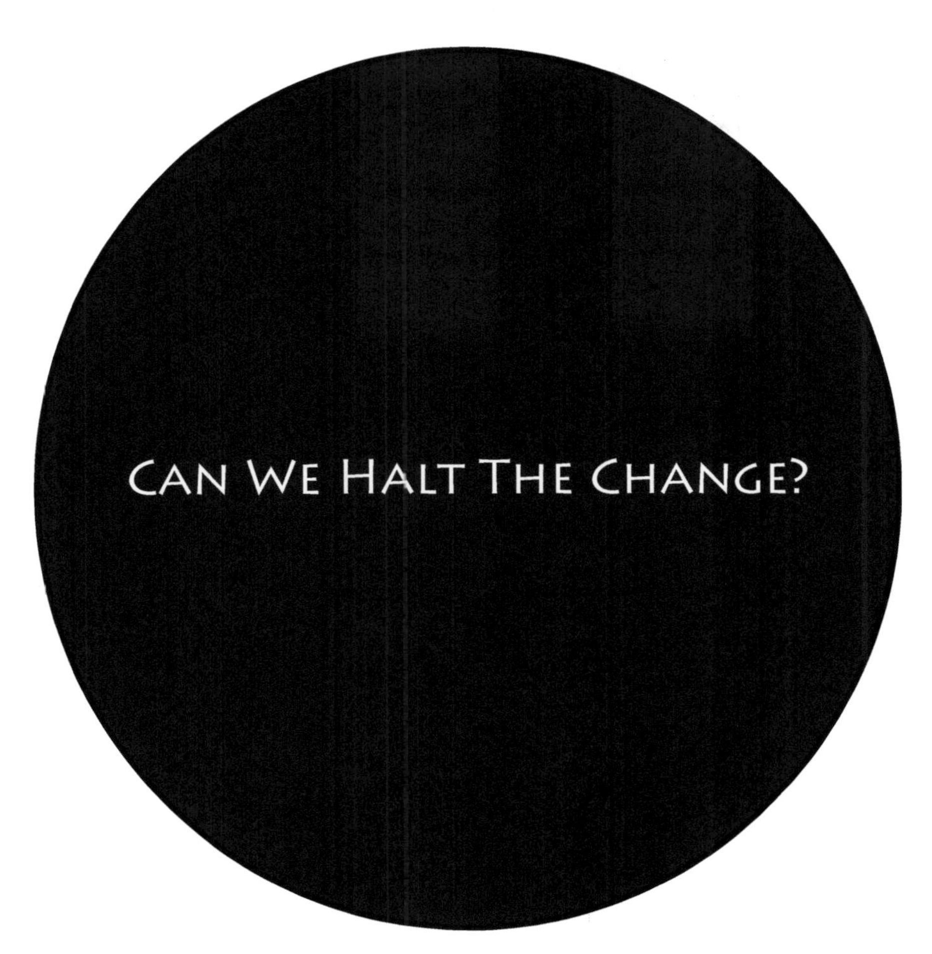
Can We Halt The Change?

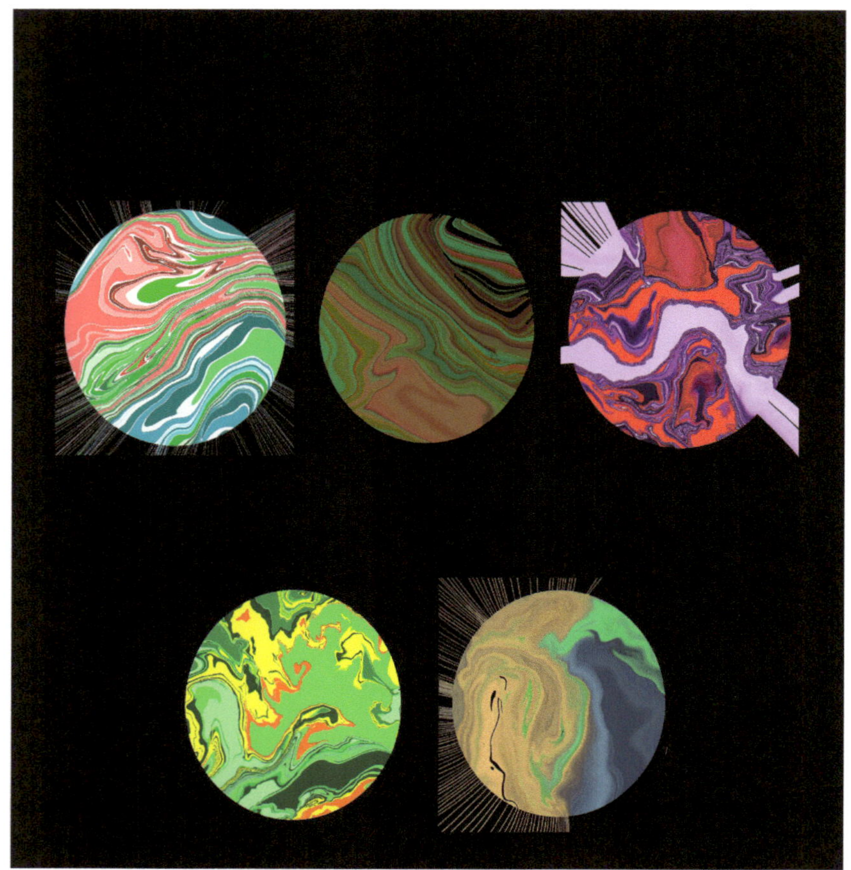

Climate emergency.

Two words of great power that we can't ignore.

Is it too late?

Can we halt the change?

Can we reverse the damage?

Creator God,
help us to accept changes in our lifestyles
needed to halt,
or hopefully reverse,
global warming.

Swans migrating south
Though warmer zones now closer
Confusing seasons

I saw two swan heads when I painted this but have to admit I can only see one now.

Birds migrate to places which are perfect for nesting and raising young. As the climate changes across the world habitats change and this impacts birds.

Have you noticed any new bird species migrating to your area? Or the decline of a native species?

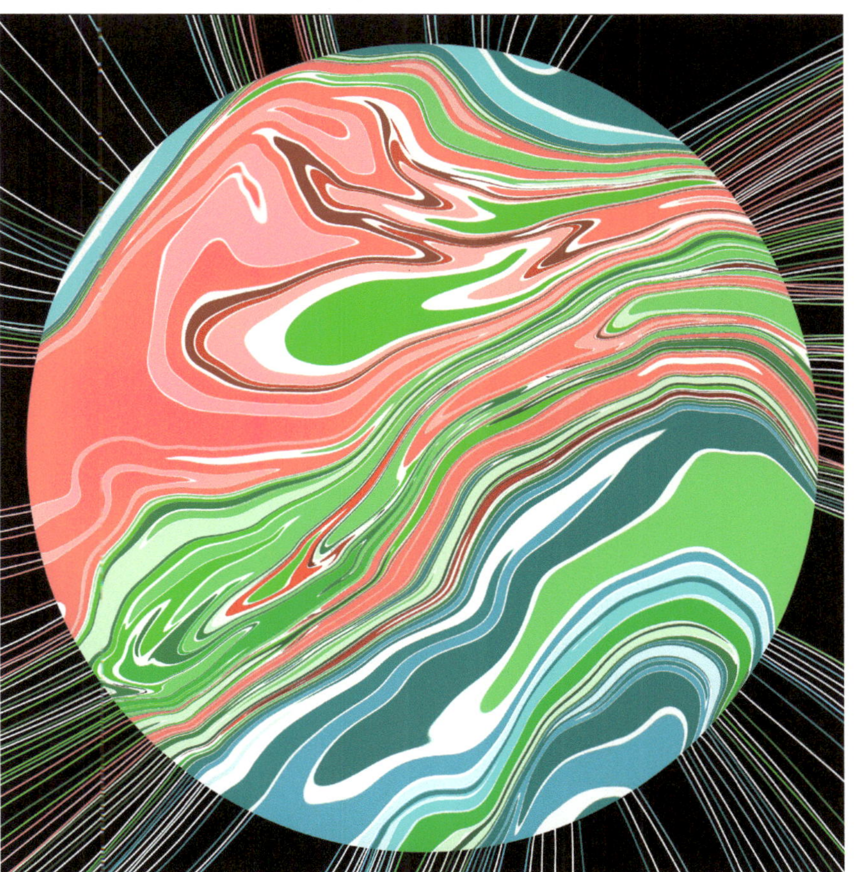

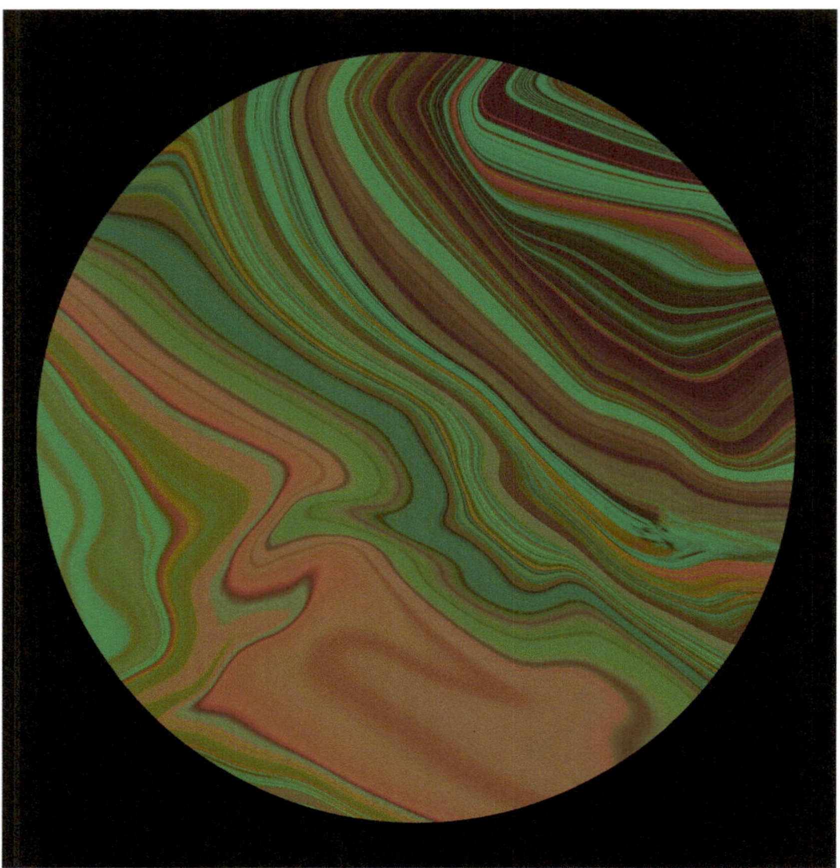

Vanishing deserts
Green not always a blessing
Can we halt the change?

Researchers have noticed for many years that deserts around the world are changing, and that the change is speeding up. Hot deserts are becoming more arid, losing as much as a third of their vegetation, while cold deserts are becoming wetter, meaning that desert species can't survive and other species grow out of control.

The ecosystem of the desert is complex and vulnerable and needs protecting.

Slowly evolving
Invading organism
What a takeover!

I created these paintings and poems during the Covid-19 pandemic. This painting and poem might easily be assumed to be about the life of a virus; but actually I'm referring to humans as the invading organism.

If the planet could talk, might it refer to us as a virus?

How does that change how we think about the planet and what we are doing to it?

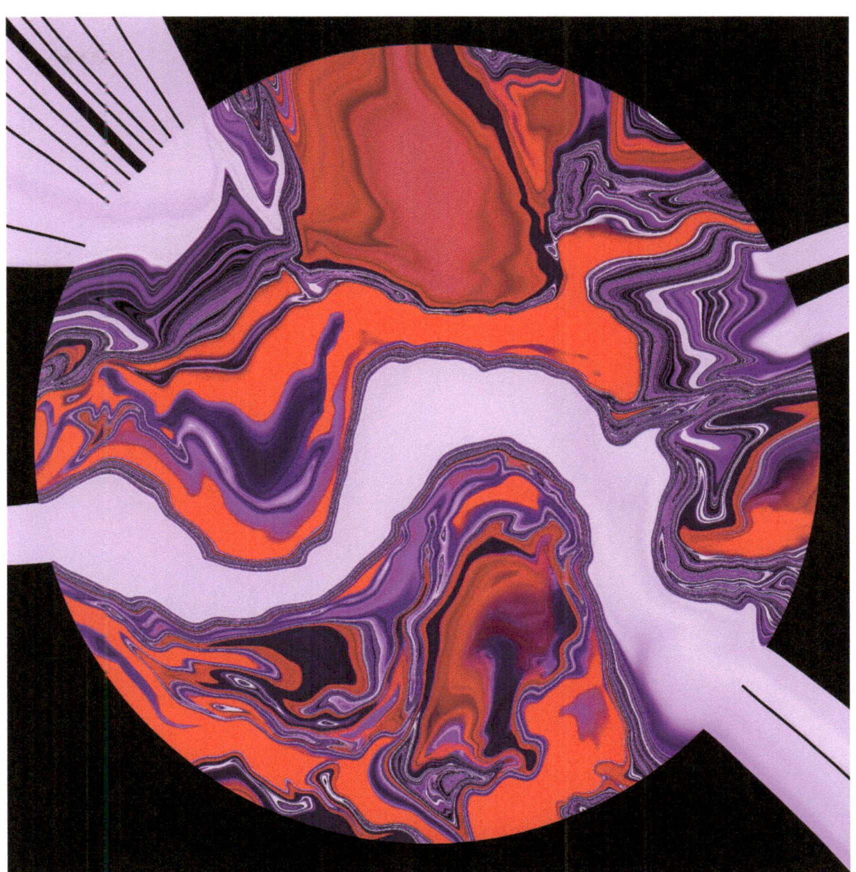

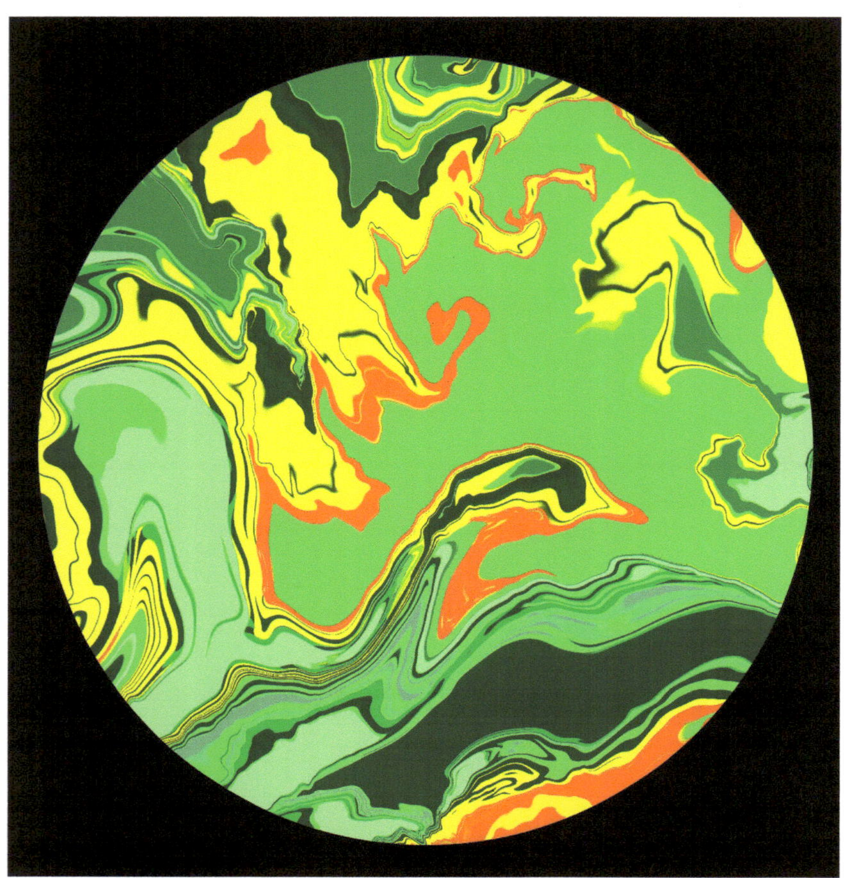

Take a bird's-eye view
We are interconnected
But ... try not to fly

I hope you can see the bird in flight in this painting. The haiku was inspired by those astronauts who have returned home and said that seeing the Earth from a distance has changed their view of the world. I wish we could all see the world that same way and come to realise that we desperately need to care for this tiny, fragile miracle of a planet.

In the haiku I'm touching on the issue of air travel. It is a difficult choice for many of us and we feel conflicted. I love to travel, to explore other cultures, to expand my horizons, but the impact of flying on the climate is huge.

How do you deal with this and other conflicts around climate change?

Coral islands wilt
Left exposed, unprotected
Beauty fades away

The death of coral reefs around the world is clear to see. But we need to remember that this is just one indicator of how much of an effect climate change is having on plants and animals around the globe.

The damage to the beauty is everywhere, even if we can't see it.

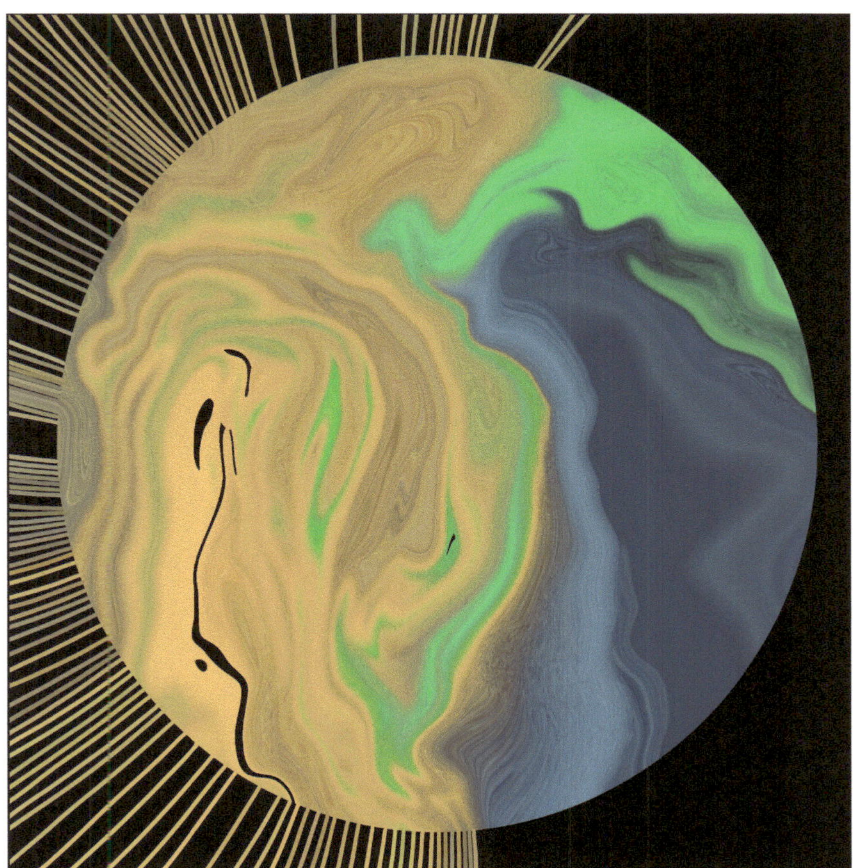

WE MUST ACT NOW!

There is hope.

We can halt the change.

We might even be able to make improvements.

But we must act now!

Creator God,
guide our decision-making,
inspire us to take action and
bring healing to the planet.

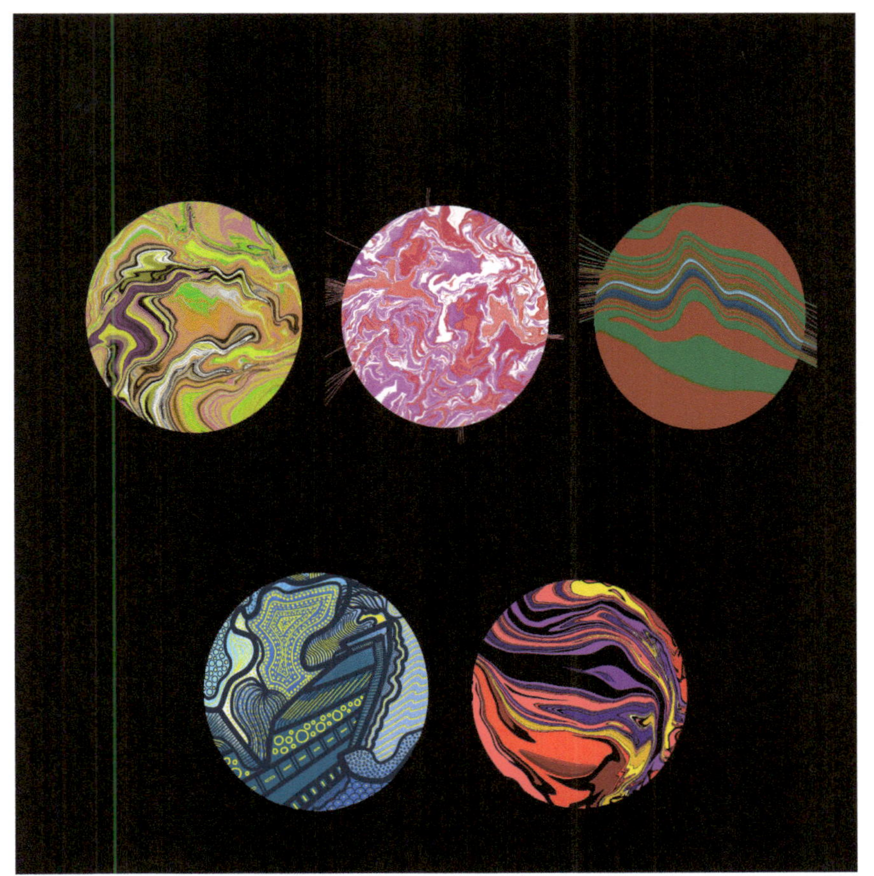

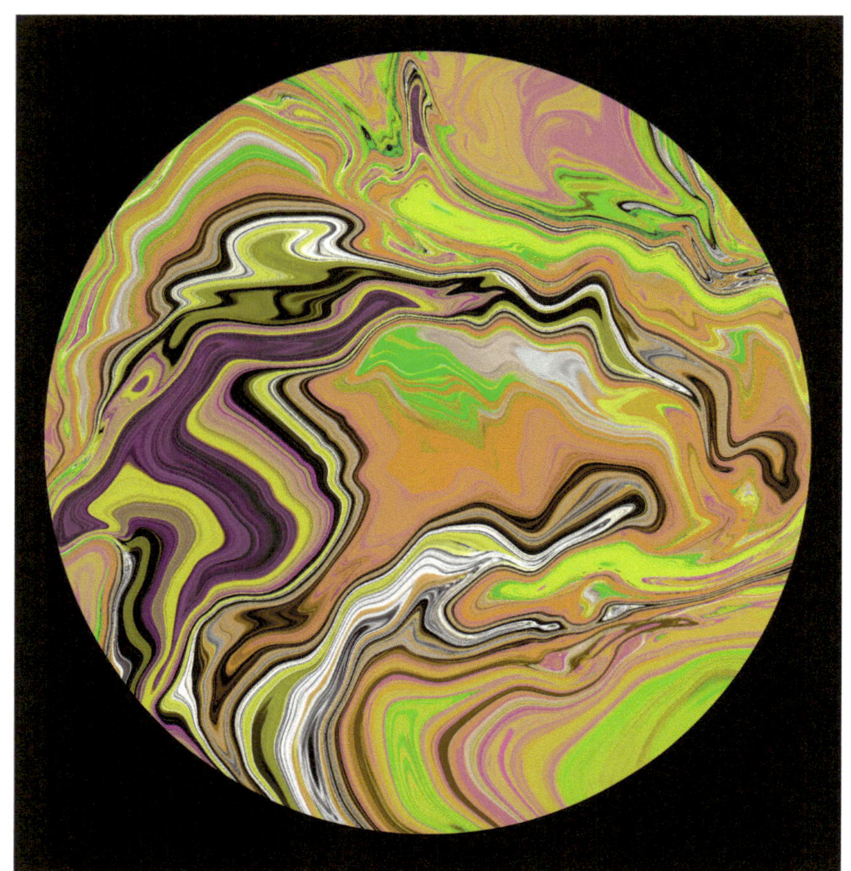

Prayers for the world
Reverse climate change damage
No hesitation

I can see two ethereal figures in prayer in this painting, on the left and right, but know most other people don't see them. After I painted this, I was immediately moved to pray *every single day* for the healing of the planet, and the poem reflects that feeling of urgency.

Who might the two figures be or symbolise, do you think?

Action reaction
Effects removed from causes
My actions matter

This painting depicts the energy in the gases at the formation of the planet. I wonder if it also depicts the angry heat that might overwhelm the world if we don't change our ways.

Every action we take, or don't take, has a reaction. My actions matter, your actions matter and, to an even greater extent, every action by companies and governments matters.

Do the companies you buy from or invest in have a commitment to reducing their impact on the environment?

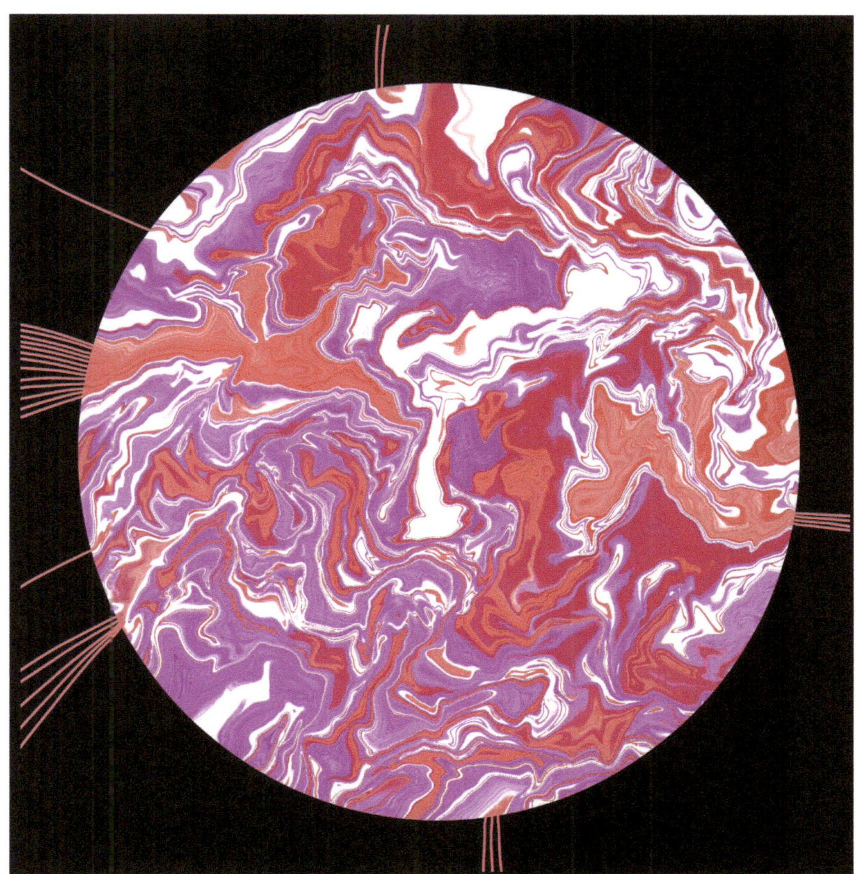

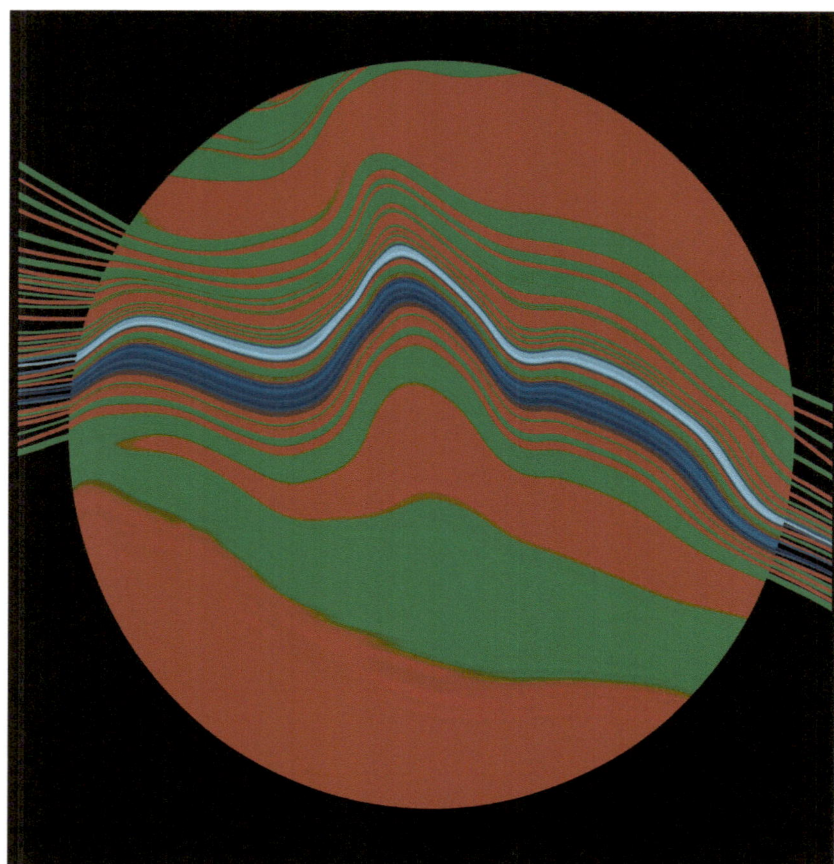

Tectonic plates shift
Impacts are catastrophic
For those without wealth

The scientific community is currently researching and debating on whether climate processes can affect the movement of the Earth's tectonic plates enough to cause an earthquake, tsunami or volcanic eruption. But there is evidence that changes in weather patterns are causing faint earth tremors known as microseisms. However, there is no debate that climate change is already having a greater impact on the poorer parts of the world, areas often prone to earthquakes, volcanos and other natural disasters.

Climate justice is about ensuring that the negative effects of climate change are distributed equally around the world and not borne predominantly by the poorest in society.

Oceanic strength
Carves complex rock formations
Together stronger

This painting is very different from all the others. I drew lines and shapes over the canvas to create this effect. When it was finished it made me think of cliffs and geological formations. Of how the same waves that gently sway sea anemones in tidepools also carve out caves and cliffs over hundreds of years.

We can apply this analogy to our lives and our impact on the planet. Every small decision to recycle or use your bicycle may seem like nothing, but together they add up to a huge force for good.

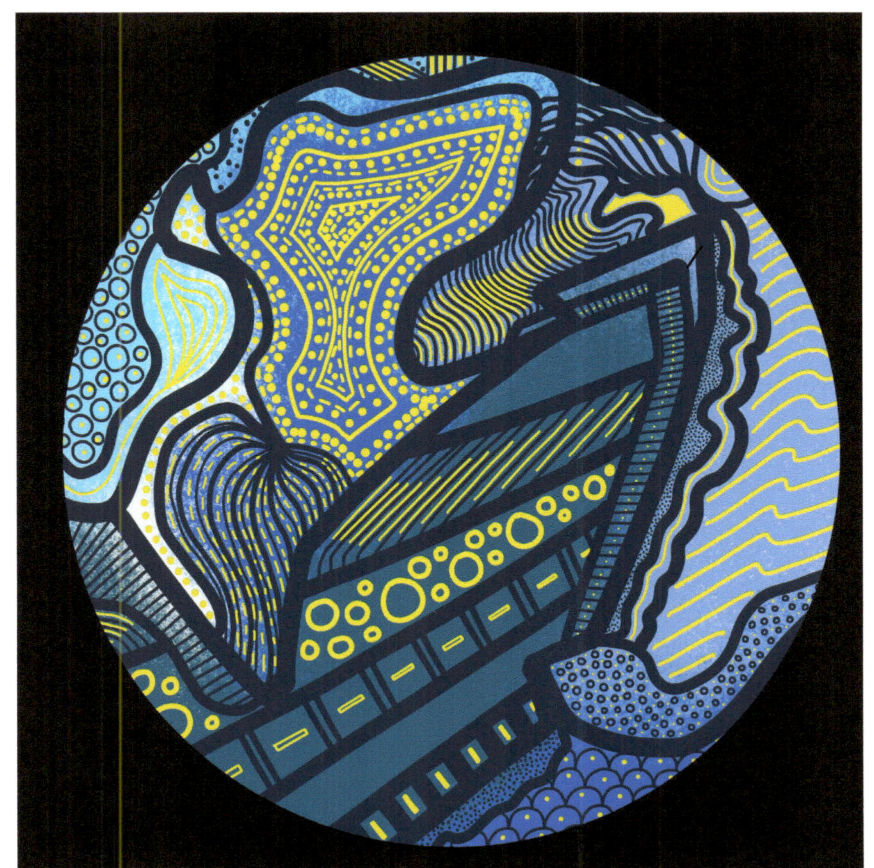

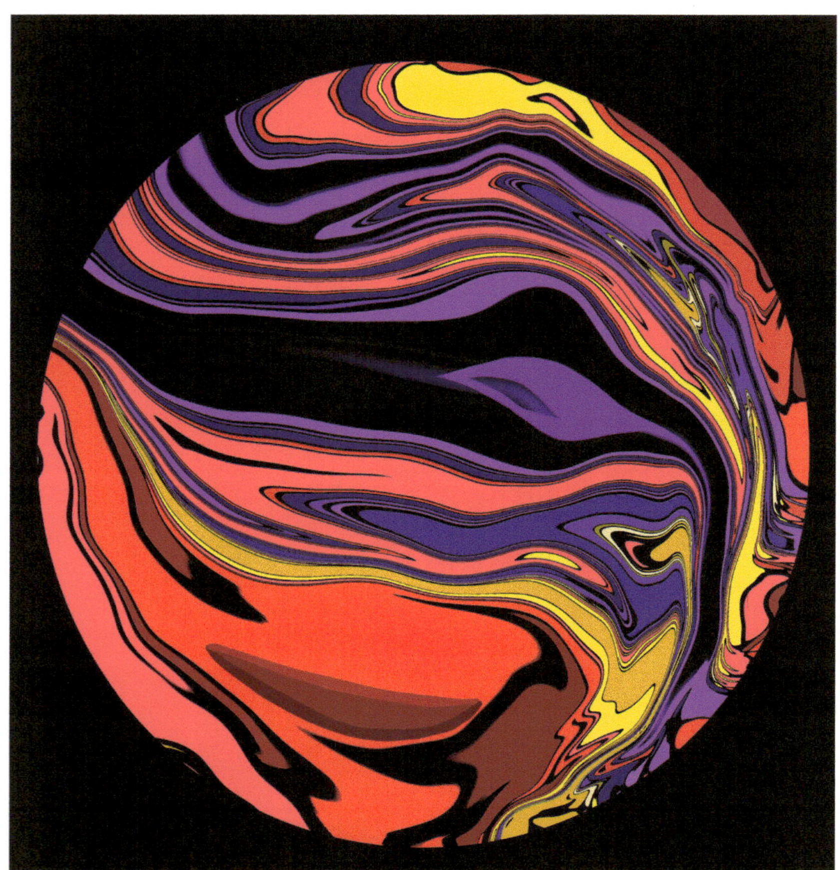

The planet's no hero
Regeneration limits
Might have been breached

I'm not going to even *try* to explain how I see a superhero in this painting. I know most of you won't see it and perhaps it's all in the eye of the creator.

For far too long we have acted as if the planet is ours for the taking and that it could never be damaged. We now know that we have caused *extensive* damage. In reality we've known this for decades. I heard it first in my GCSE geography class – and that was over 30 years ago.

I pray, every day, that regeneration limits haven't been breached, that it isn't too late to make things right and that my children's children won't read about the failure of our generation to save the planet.

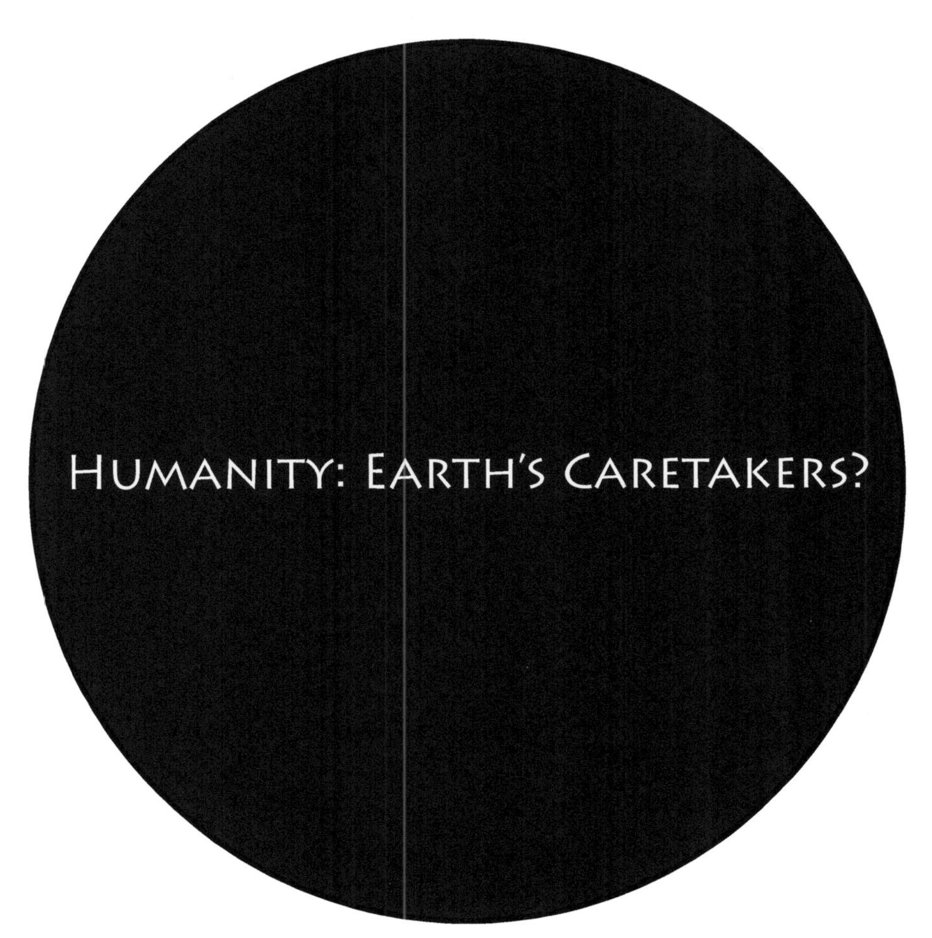

Humanity: Earth's Caretakers?

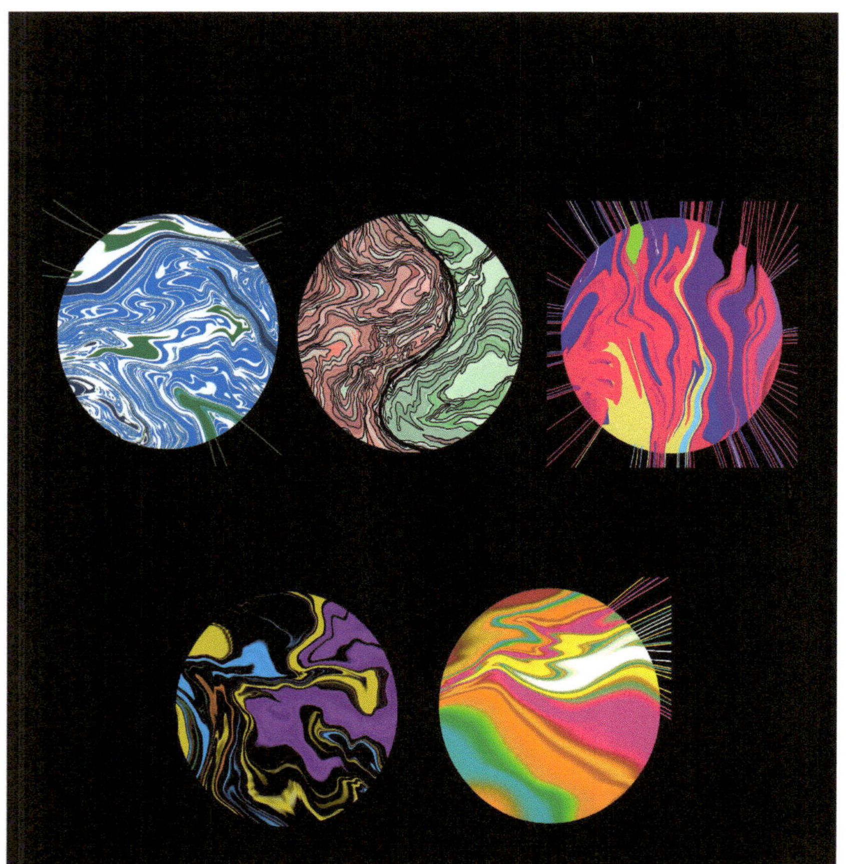

We are not entitled to use resources without considering the impact of their use. We are not the owners of the world and all that lives in it.

We are merely caretakers of the planet. How does it feel to know that your primary job is to look after the world?

Creator God,
forgive us our failings,
give us words to inspire others,
focus our minds on the future.

Human arrogance
The world is not our oyster
We are caretakers

Arrogance is a strong word, isn't it? But I think it fits the bill.

I think we, as a species, have put ourselves above all other animals. We believe that we are better, cleverer, more civilised, and therefore more entitled. But what we forget in this thinking is that we literally can't survive without every other living thing on the planet.

For example, when we spray insecticides on crops or even on our gardens, we decimate the insect population which we need to pollinate our plants.

We need to work with the natural world rather than against it.

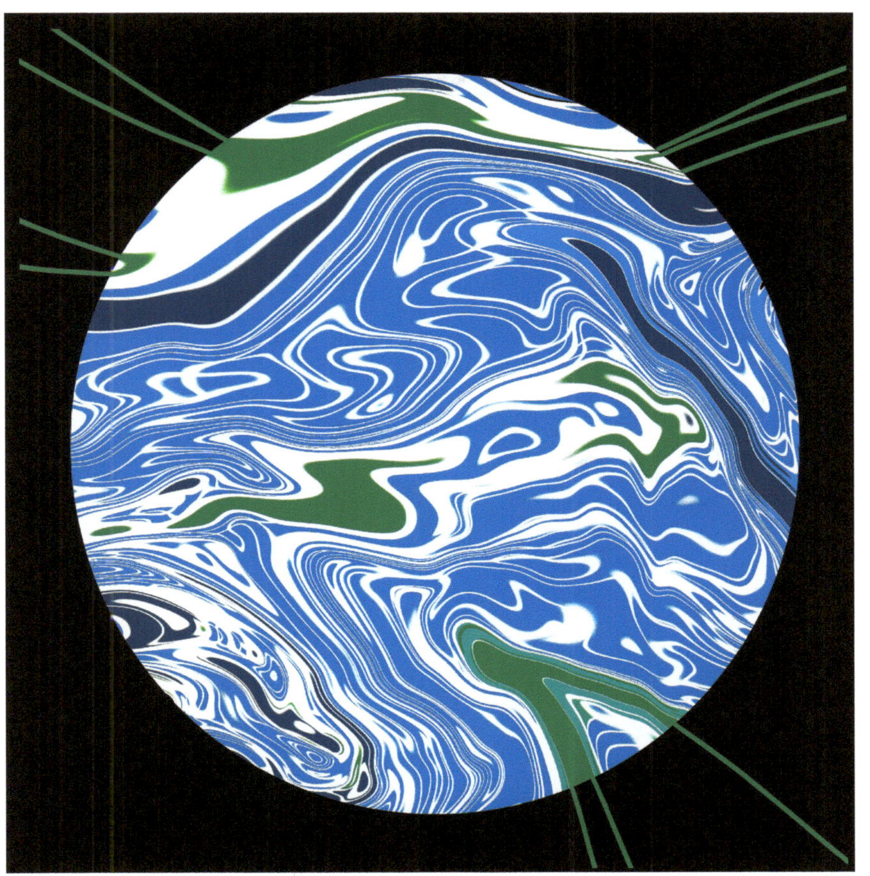

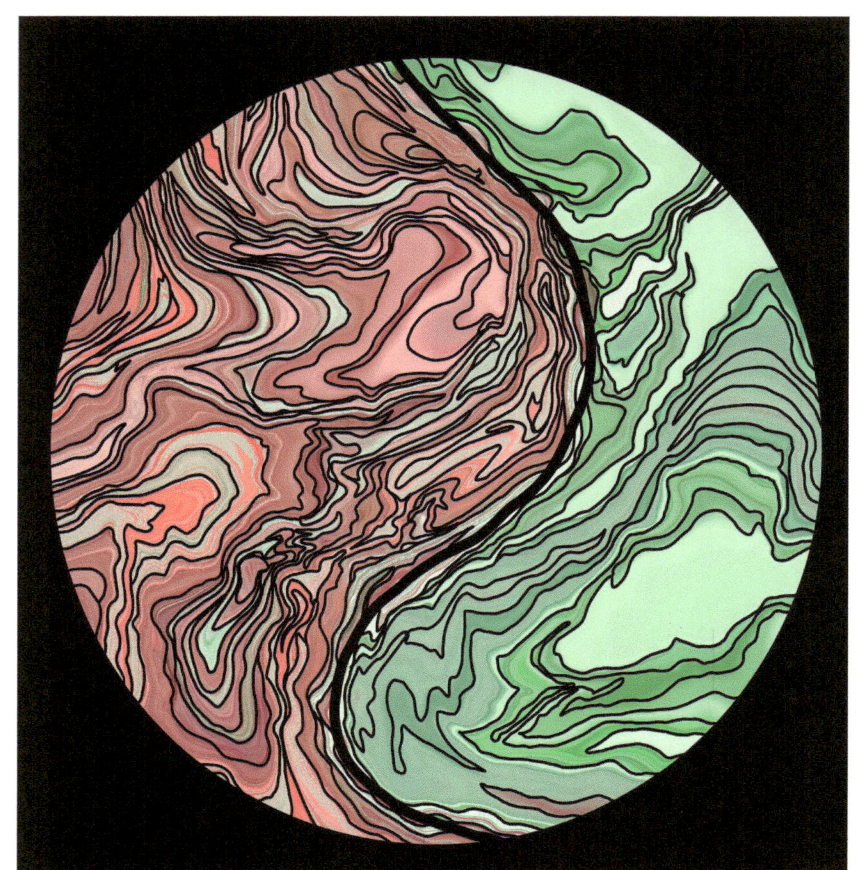

Balancing actions
Is compromise possible
Or does green fight greed?

For many years the climate lobby has been seen as in opposition to big business and governments. One wants to reduce the impact of humans upon the planet, the other wants profits and wealth.

In the last few years this view seems to be changing, although there's still a long way to go. It is only by listening, understanding, compromising and finding ways to work together that we can tackle the climate emergency. We must all consider our priorities, evaluate our decisions and take appropriate action.

Planet on fire
Creation regenerates
If given a chance

In 2020, Australia saw the worst wildfires in living memory; in 2021, Canada and the USA experienced extreme temperatures and their own awful wildfires. There is no doubt that this is climate change in action and that these extreme events have focused minds around the world.

In this painting and haiku I was thinking about the amazing ways that plants regenerate after natural fires, of the ways that fire can be beneficial for certain species which had been suffocated by others becoming too dominant. I am holding on to the optimistic view that if we work together then we can stop the fire of climate change and regenerate the world in a more balanced way.

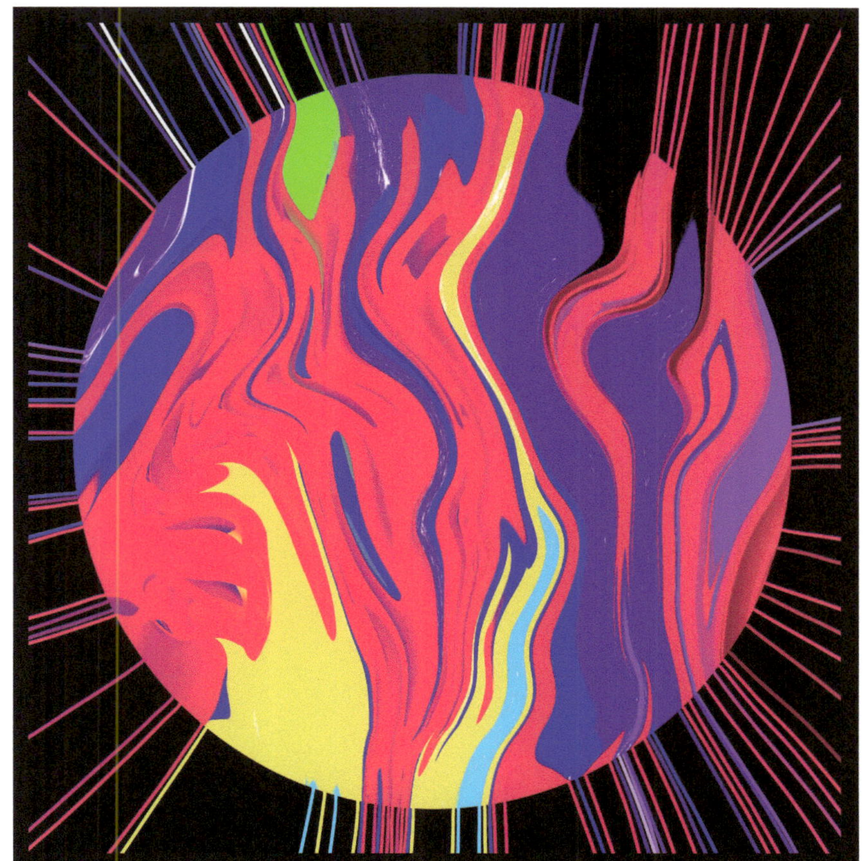

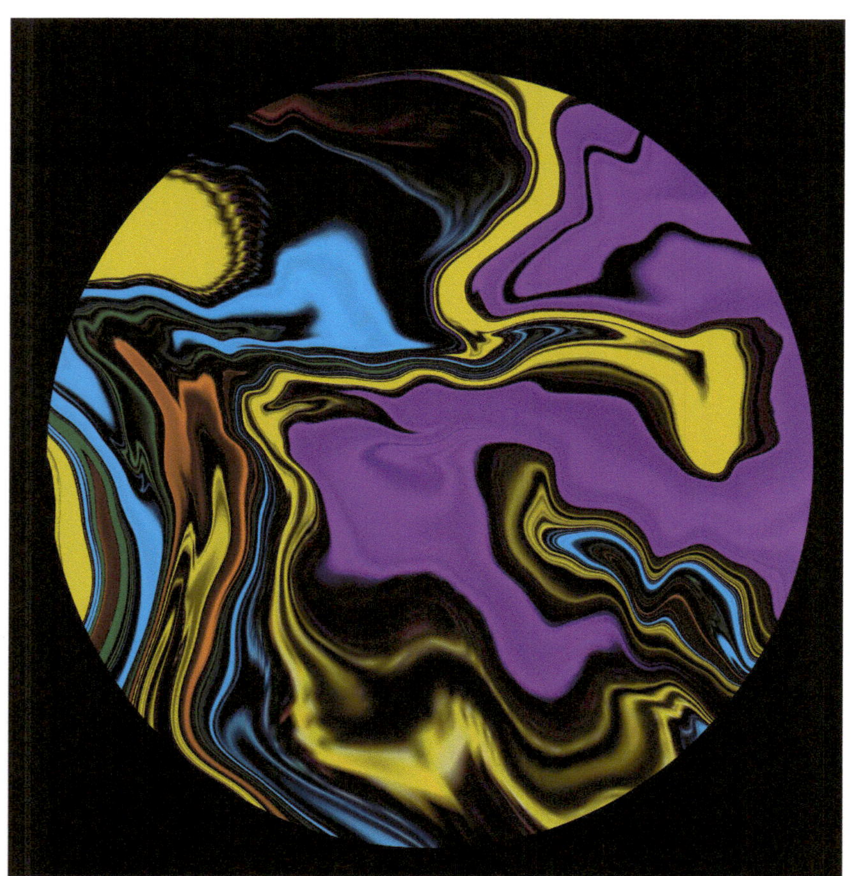

Across the planet
Let differences drop away
One human species

Humans and bananas share 60% of the same DNA. Humans and chimpanzees share 98%. Yet we view ourselves as different and other. Even as communities we find it hard to find our similarities – let alone across countries. If we are going to find a solution to the climate emergency then we need to realise that we are all in this together.

The decisions will not be easy, but they are necessary. There will be pain on all sides, and that must be borne more by the richer countries than the poorest.

Most of you reading this will likely be living in one of the richer countries. Are you willing to feel some pain for the good of earth's community?

Our lights pollute
Nature's circadian clock
Rhythms out of time

Are you old enough to remember how dark it used to be at night and how many stars there were in the sky? Perhaps you live somewhere without light pollution. I don't – and love the darkness of night in more rural places.

The differences between day and night are important for every organism on earth. Species have evolved to be active during the day or at night. Light pollution is increasing around the world and impacting on animals, who can no longer even tell if it's day or night.

Do we need as much light at night? Each light source needs power to fuel it and much of that has a carbon footprint.

Could we turn down the lights to see the stars?

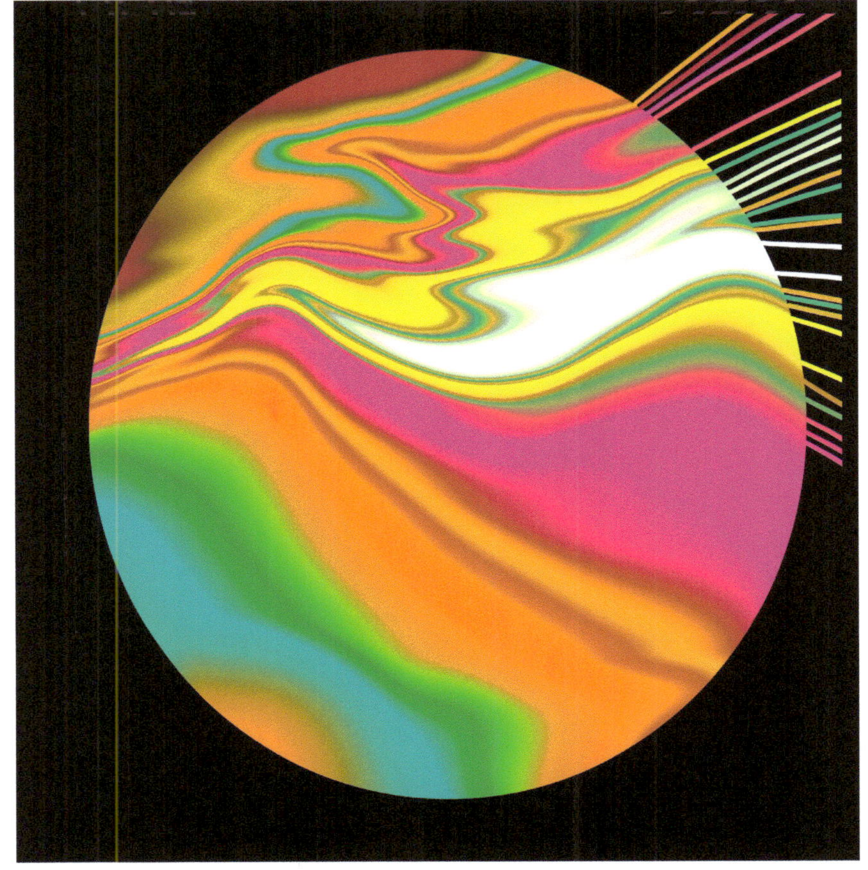

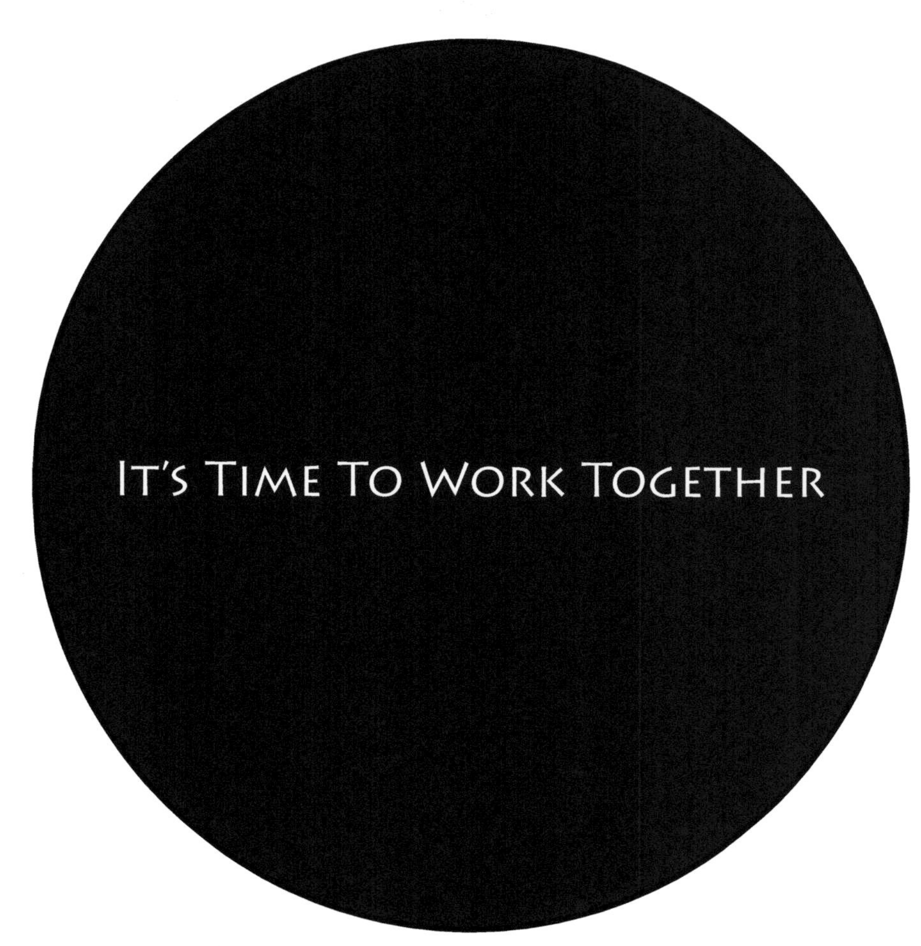
IT'S TIME TO WORK TOGETHER

It's time to put our differences aside.

It's time to find solutions together.

It's time to think globally.

Creator God,
be in the rooms
where ideas are generated,
possibilities are considered
and solutions are created.

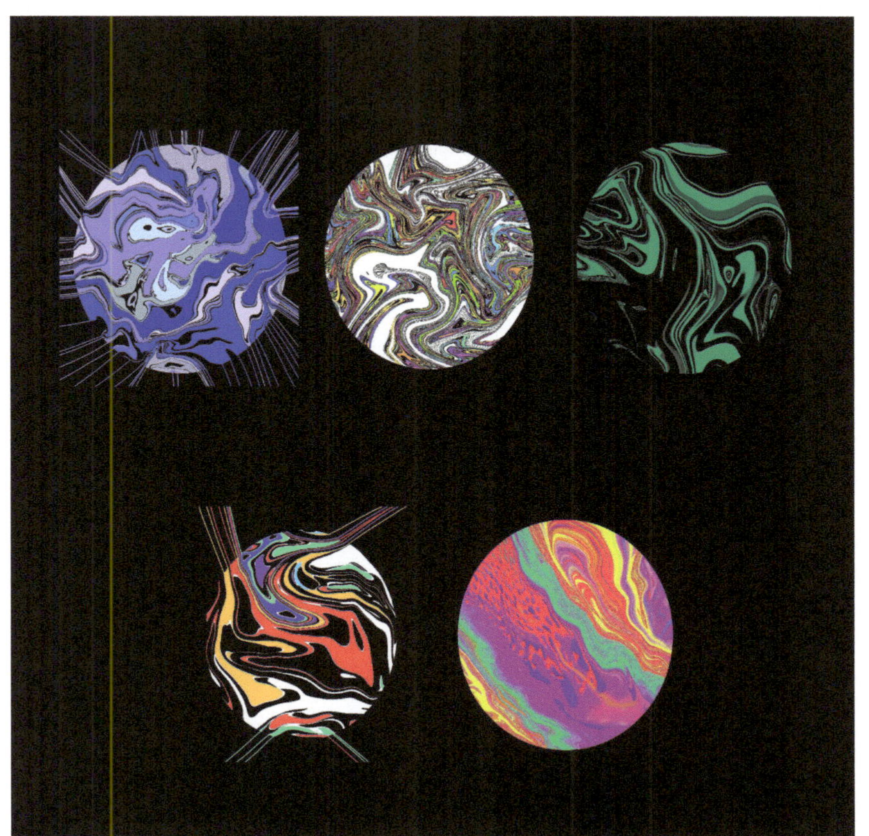

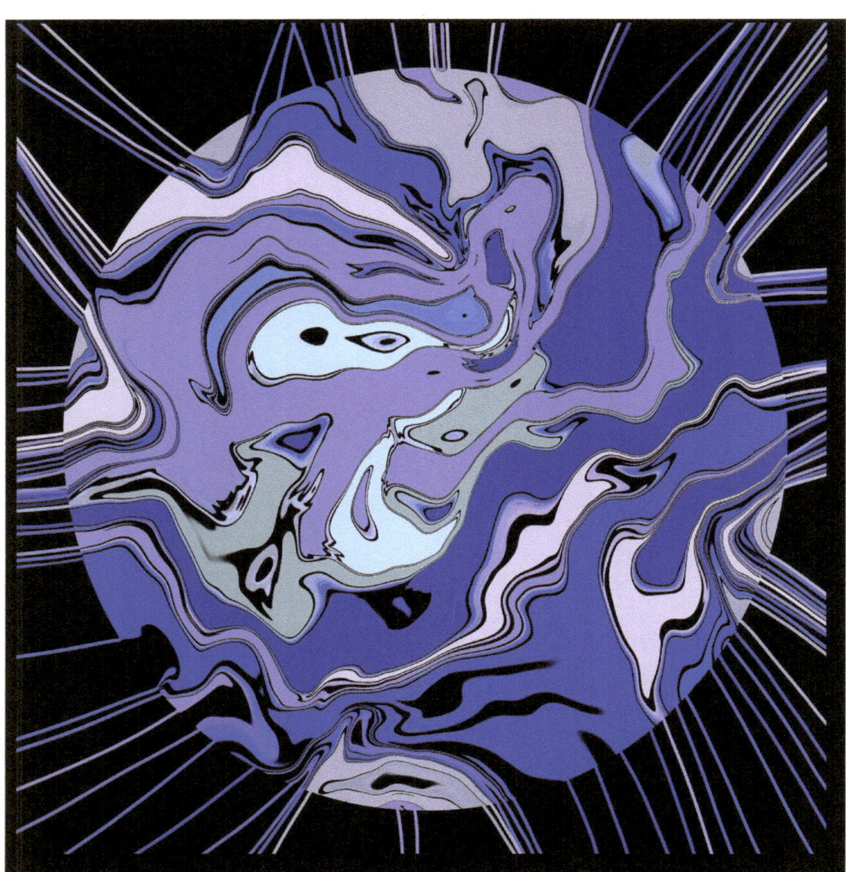

Water limited
A closed circuit for us all
Share volume fairly

When I was in primary school there was a competition by the local water authority to design a poster to reduce water use. I drew a picture of a bath with three elephants in it with the slogan: 'Save water, bath with a friend!'

The fact that there is a limited supply of water is not new news. The fact that many people around the world still don't have access to clean water is not new news either.

What can you do to reduce your use of water this week?

Exploring icebergs
Millennia on the move
Melting time bombs tick

The ice sheets in the Arctic and Antarctic are melting. Icebergs are breaking off – the current largest is four times the size of New York. It's hard to imagine anything that big floating around. Now try to imagine that melting and raising water levels around the world.

Do you know which parts of your local area might be underwater in 50 years' time? It's a reality check.

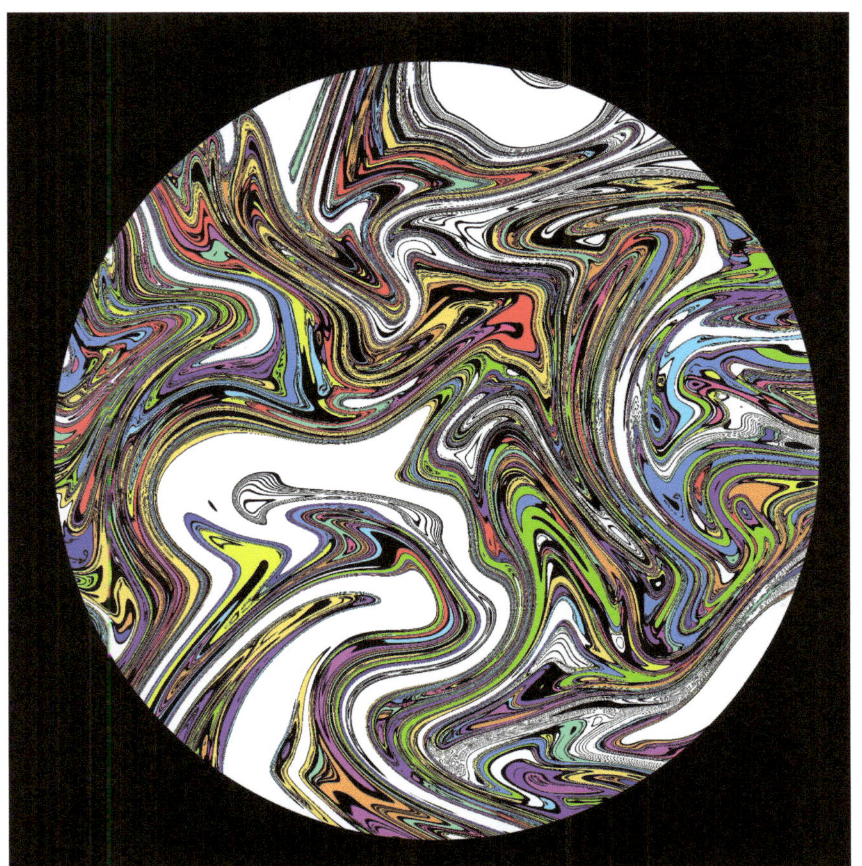

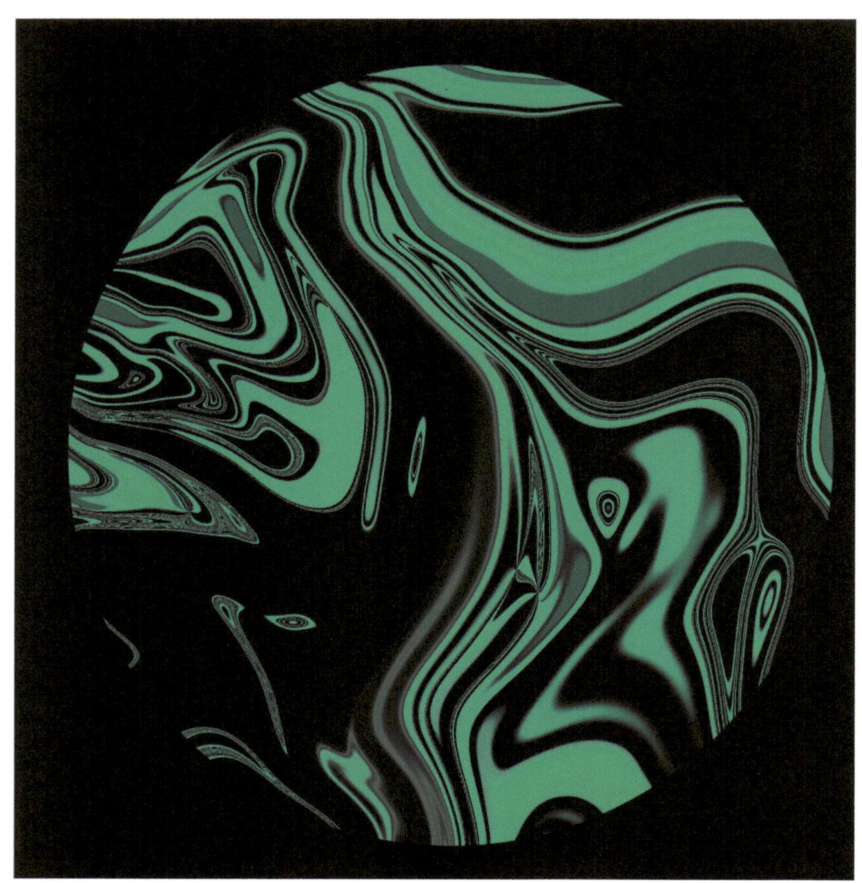

In between the green
Nature is decimated
Scorched earth needing care

This is a stark painting: a vision of what might become, with our oceans turned sickly green with pollution and our lands burned black.

I pray that this painting is merely a figment of my imagination.

Ideas emerge
Converge, strengthen, expand
Greater than their parts

But let's think positively.

Let's imagine what will happen when those in power finally work together to find solutions.

Think positively. Imagine …

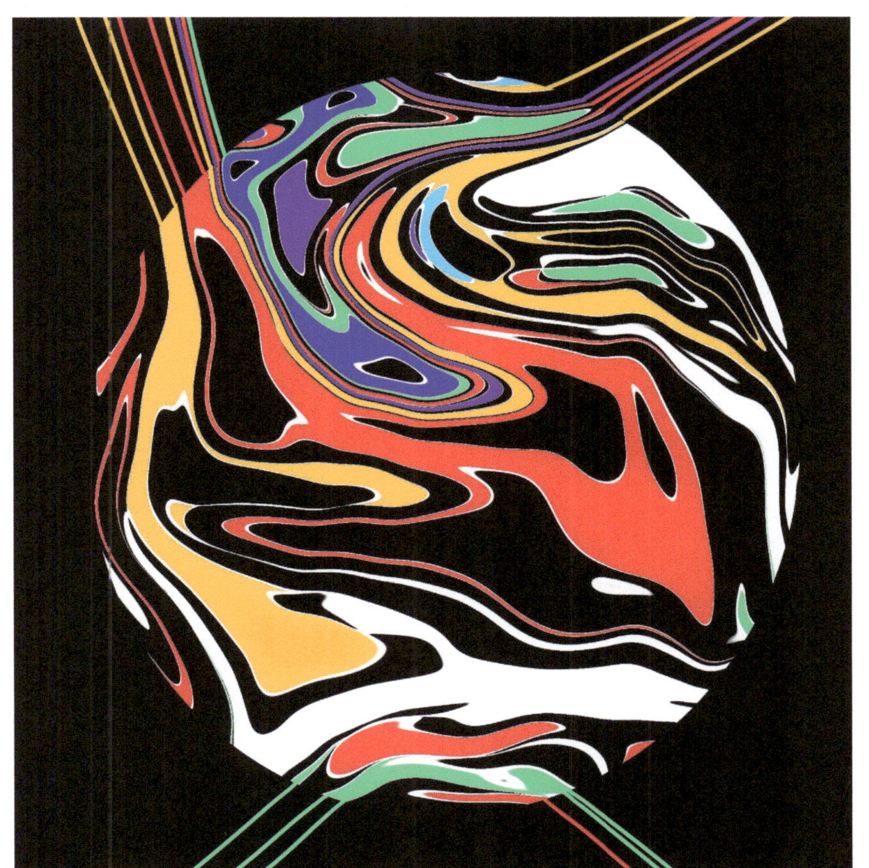

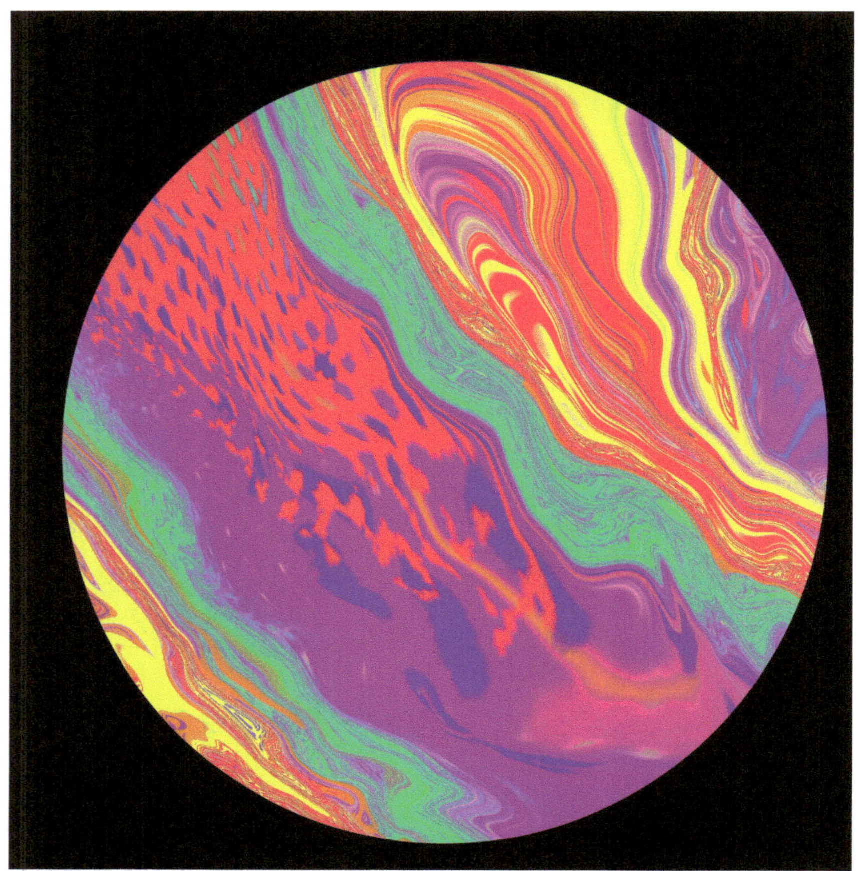

Follow the current
Finding solutions for change
Moving together

I love the way this painting seems to move, to flow …

It made me think about how, if we all move in the same direction, amazing things can happen.

The key is to do it together, supporting and encouraging each other …

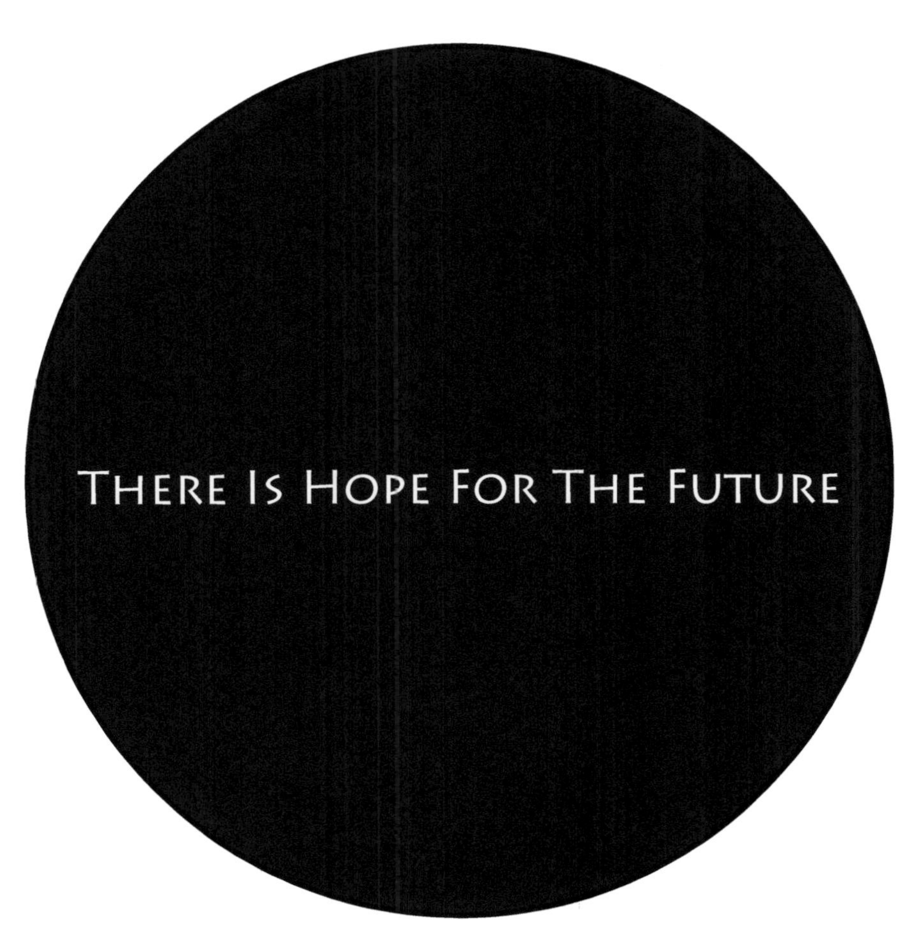
There Is Hope For The Future

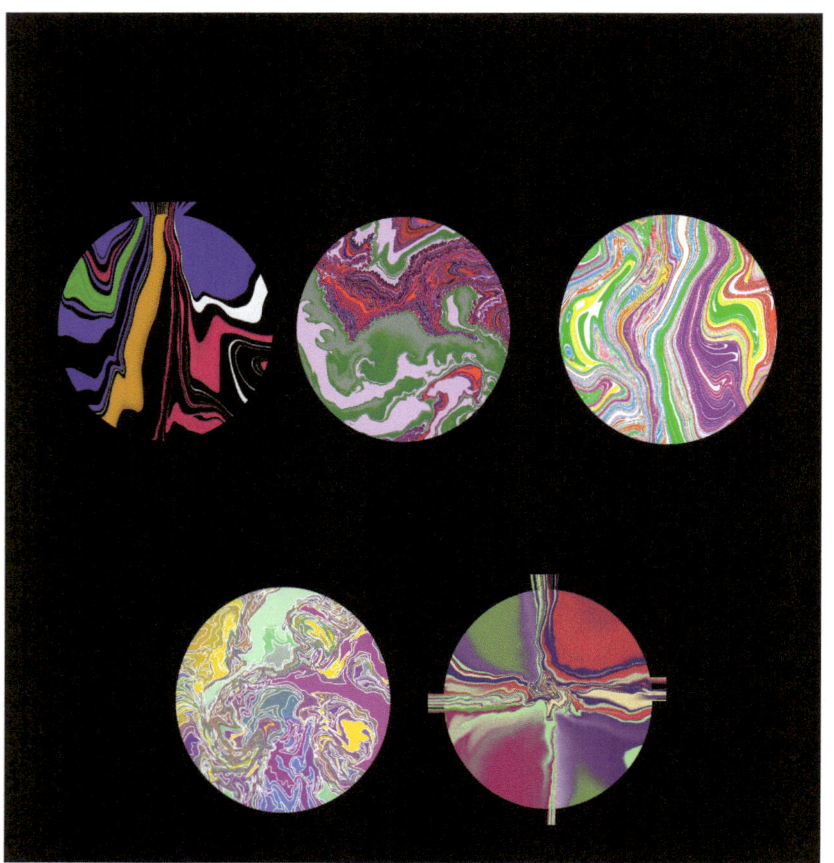

There is hope. There is always hope.

Scientists are researching. Engineers are designing. Inventors are inventing. Economists are calculating. Lawyers are incentivising. Young people are inspiring. People are acting.

There is hope. There is always hope.

Creator God,
thank you for the young people
who lead the way
in demanding change;
help us hear them,
be inspired by them
and engage with them.

Under huge pressure
Humanity's heavy load
Something's gotta give

Something is going to give if we keep on living the way we are. Either we'll pass the point of no return or those with power will finally realise that things must change.

My prayer is that it's the latter – and I'm doing all I can to make that happen by contacting politicians, joining activist groups, by creating paintings, poems and writing this book.

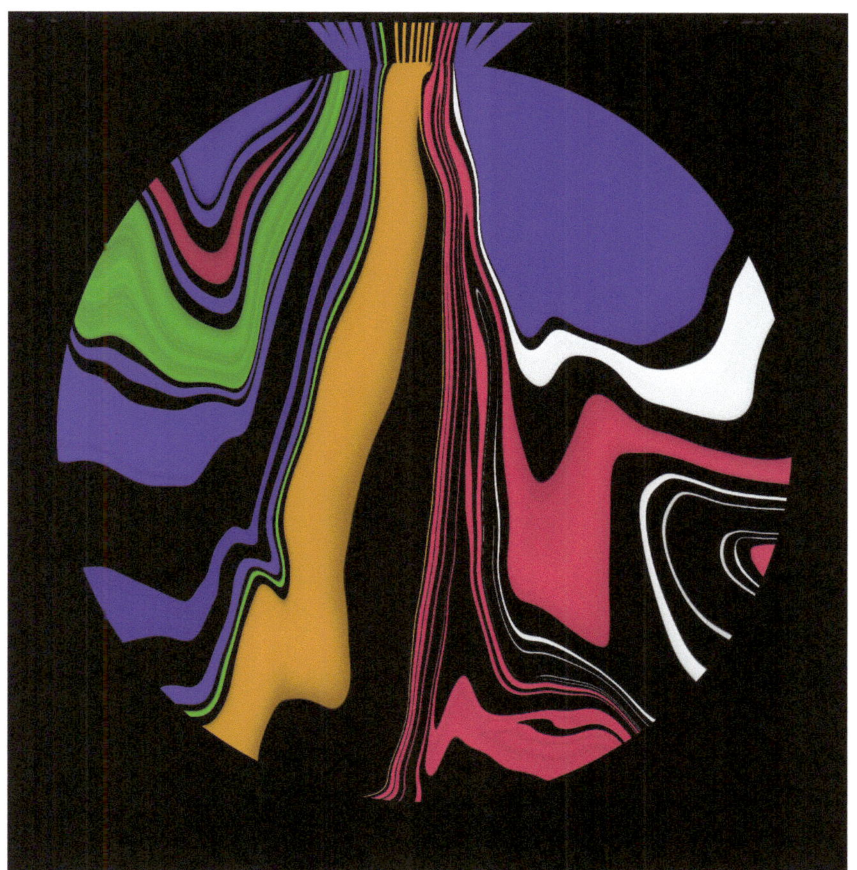

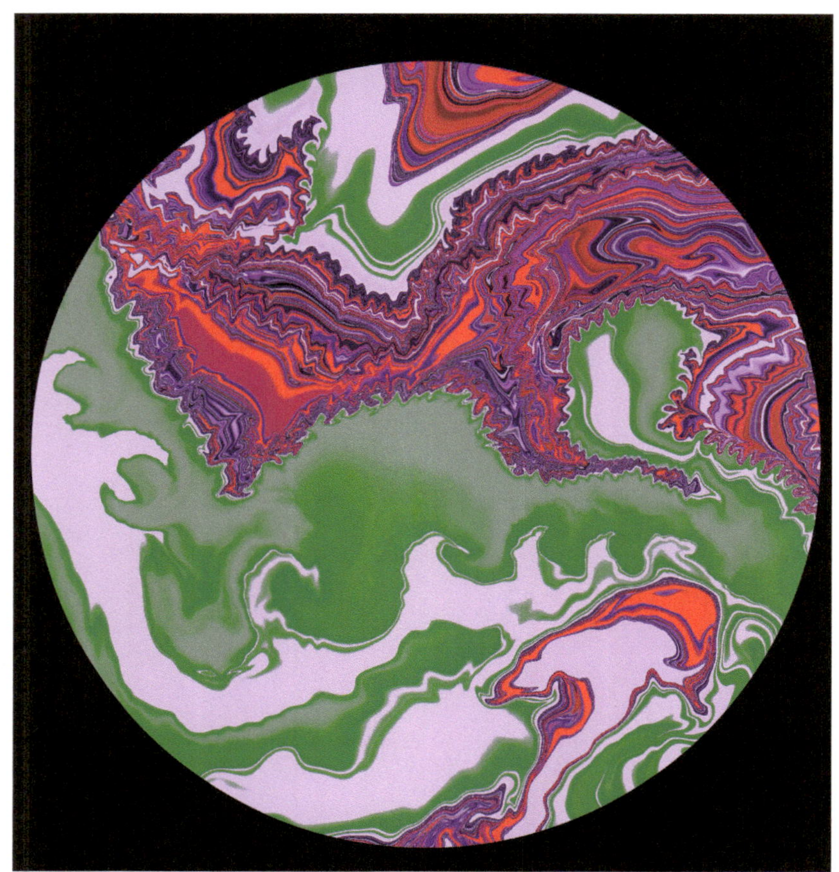

Science digs deeper
Seeking true causality
Beneath climate change

If anyone is going to find out how we can reverse the impact of climate change, then it will be the scientists. People observing and researching the way the world works and what is changing. Scientists will find the exact causes of climate-change damage and share this with engineers, who can find solutions.

Searching for problems
Developing solutions
Planning together

I'm an engineer by background: we are problem-solvers. We never do this alone; we work in groups, bringing together different skills and experience.

Engineers are redesigning machines and processes to reduce technology's impact on the environment. They are designing better ways of harnessing solar, wind, wave and geothermal energy. They are working on ideas we haven't even heard of yet!

As consumers we need to be ready to change the way we live, thanks to the problem-solving skills of engineers.

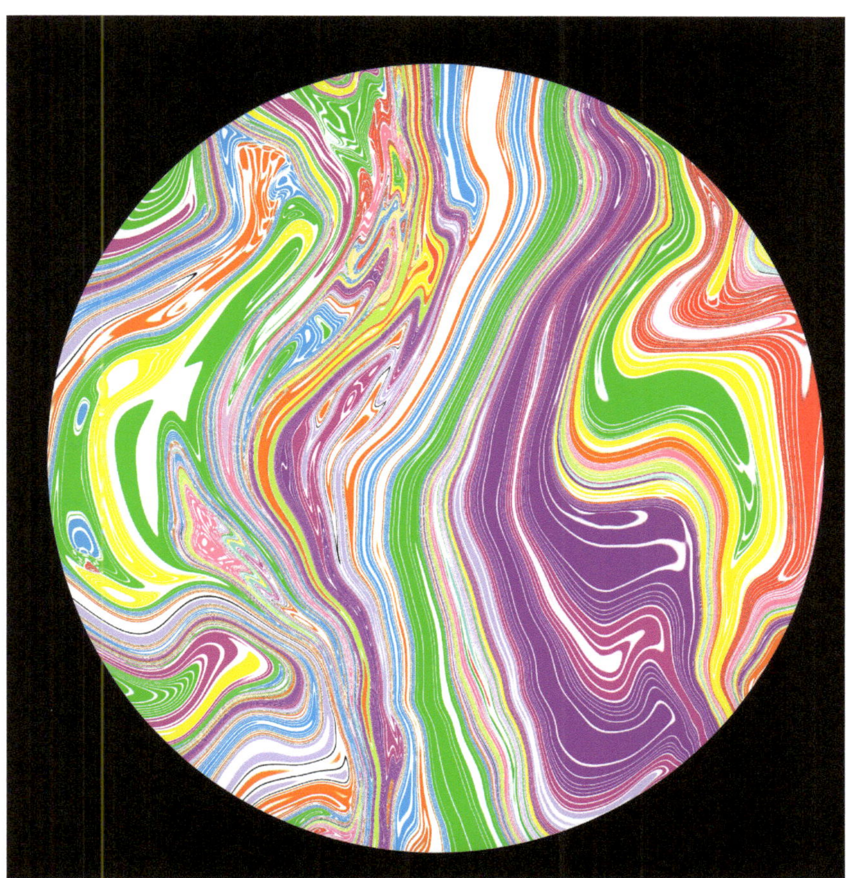

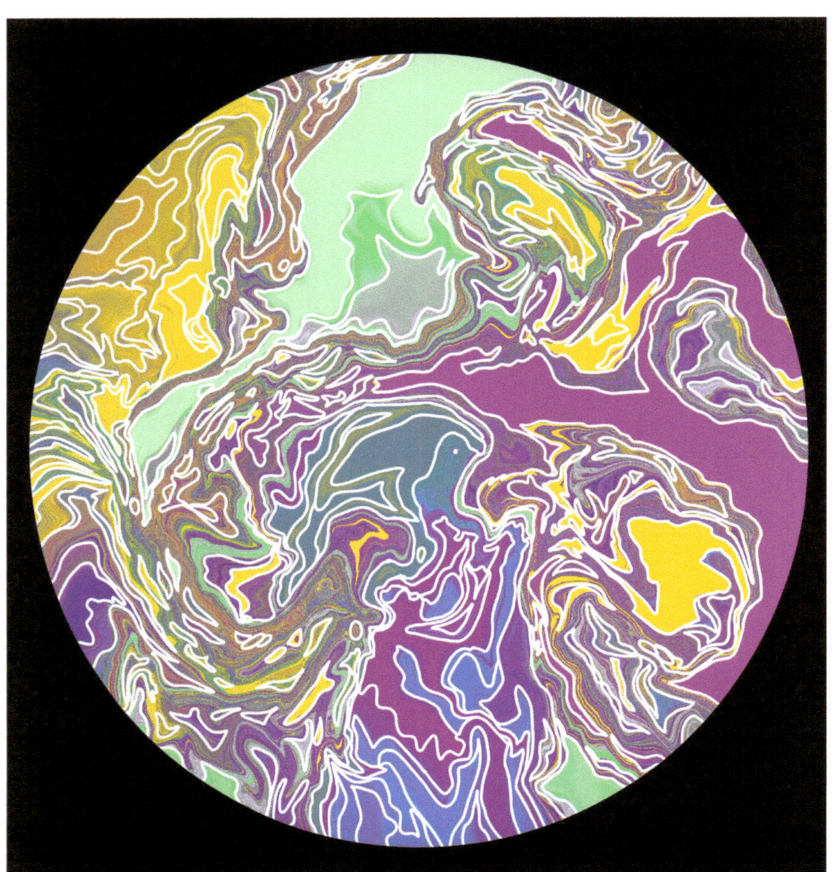

You make me believe
There is hope for the future
You will change the world

I wrote this thinking about the many young people I know. They inspire me in their care for the world, their determination to make things better and their enthusiasm that change is possible.

When people tell me that the youth of today aren't interested in politics, I tell them to go and meet some *actual* young people, because they give me hope.

Care for creation
A task for every nation
Together let's act

In November 2021 leaders from around the world met in Glasgow at COP26 to make plans to tackle climate change. There were some positive developments – but much more needs to be done.

Let's continue to surround world leaders in prayer as they continue to listen, discuss, debate and plan the way forward to combat the climate emergency.

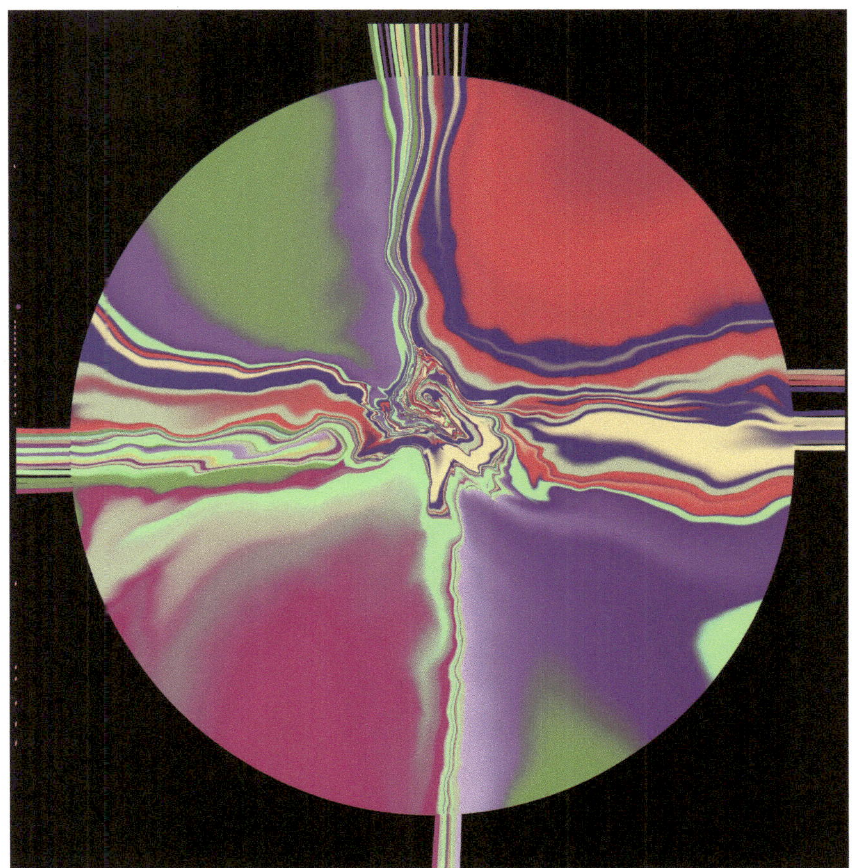

And so we find ourselves at the end of a journey
about climate justice.

I wonder which of the paintings sticks in your
mind?

Is there a haiku which particularly spoke to you?

Have you felt inspired in any way?

Where will you go from here?

I hope you will revisit this book again and again, to
be reminded of the issues and inspired to take
another small action, because they all help.